THE MODERN RULES OF

RULES OF

Personal

Finance

FOR PROFESSIONALS

THE MODERN RULES SERIES

The Modern Rules of Order

The Modern Rules of Style

The Modern Rules of Personal Finance

The Modern Rules of Business Etiquette

THE MODERN RULES OF
Personal Finance

FOR PROFESSIONALS

SUSAN A. BERSON

Defending Liberty
Pursuing Justice

Library of Congress Cataloging-in-Publication Data

Berson, Susan A.
   The modern rules of personal finance.
   Susan A. Berson
Library of Congress Cataloging-in-Publication Data is on file.

ISBN: 978-1-59031-923-9

Table of Contents

Introduction.. vii

Chapter 1
Financial Goals:
From Debt-Free to Retiring Early 1

Chapter 2
The "B" Word: Everyone Needs a Budget................ 13

Chapter 3
Student Loan Debt:
The Good, the Bad, and the Ugly 33

Chapter 4
Credit: How to Use It Wisely................................. 53

Chapter 5
Housing: It's Not How Much Mortgage
You Qualify For, but How Much You
Can Comfortably Afford to Pay 75

Chapter 6
When Your Iceberg Melts:
Insuring for Catastrophes 89

Chapter 7
Investment Basics 111

Chapter 8
Taxes.. 135

Chapter 9
Retirement Planning 149

Chapter 10
Life Events 165

Chapter 11
Giving Back 183

Appendix A
Spender Quiz:
What Kind of Spender Are You? 189

Appendix B
Financial "To Do" Checklist 197

About the Author 199

Index 200

Introduction

Dedicated to those who are prosperous in spirit, may you soon have the portfolio to match.

Financially speaking, most young professionals either feel smothered by student loan and credit card debt, or euphoric at being flush with cash from a hefty paycheck, preparing to engage in mass consumerism and purchase all the accoutrements of wealth their hard work deserves. There are even a few who feel fortunate at being already wealthy—though not super-rich yet. No matter where you stand on this spectrum, this book is for you. Common to everyone is the oft-quoted axiom, "people don't plan to fail, they fail to plan." That's true with financial success. By the way, the fly-by-the-seat-of-your-pants attitude, vowing to save next year, is not a plan. It eventually leads to financial problems, whether you're earning $60,000 or $1 million. When you become financially strapped, work—no matter how glamorous or prestigious—can seem more like a dungeon than a career.

The purpose of this book is to help you learn how to manage what you can control: your money. Effective money management is the tool that is going to help you find the means to achieve your dreams. After graduation, you begin at the helm of a glorious ship that's sailing off into a very beautiful sunset—but it's very important that you know what route you're going to follow.

The advice in this book is based on those who have sailed these waters before. The ideas offered could guarantee you a financially successful voyage. But it depends on you. Will you work to fund a financial lifestyle or create financial independence? The price for financial independence can be as little as 10 percent of your paycheck every month. For those who are drowning in debt and feel as though they'll never stay afloat, don't be discouraged. Remember that part of success is believing that you can do anything you set your mind to do—think of the billions amassed by Oprah Winfrey, Robert Redford and Warren Buffett. Sure, your inner monologue says, they're all unique, but that only explains *why* they made money, not *how* they were able to retain and grow their wealth when others in their industries have lost or squandered their earnings. Armed with the sound financial practices in this book, achieving your financial goals will become milestones, not end points. There is a *multi*-millionaire inside you, it just requires learning to effectively manage your spending and saving habits, as well as risk and contingency planning.

Financial Goals:
From Debt-Free to Retiring Early

"Without goals, and plans to reach them, you are like a ship that has set sail with no destination."
Fitzhugh Dodson

When it comes to finances, it's important to be the captain of your own ship. Many professionals set career goals, but put little energy into charting their financial goals. Where you are in life's events will dictate what you need and want and, thus, what your financial goals should be. For example, most recent graduates may have paying off their students loans as a number-one priority. Seasoned working professionals, on the other hand, might be more interested in the goal of retiring early. Surprisingly, very few professionals, young or seasoned, take the time to chart out the financial goals (between becoming debt-free and retiring early) that crop up when life events occur . When it comes to your finances, winging it will not produce a positive result. Diagramming your financial goals, and a corresponding plan to achieve them, is key to achieving life-long financial prosperity.

1

Drafting a blueprint for your financial prosperity involves three steps: (1) assessing your present financial condition; (2) determining your financial goals; and (3) developing a strategy to meet your goals. So, before doing anything else, assess where you are financially in life by preparing a balance sheet. List everything you own on one side of the page, and all debt on the other side. Then, add up each side of the page, and subtract all your liabilities from your total assets to arrive at your net worth. The Net Worth Balance Worksheet can help you.

Liabilities (What You Owe)

Home Mortgage/other Real Estate Loans (balance owed)	_____
Credit Cards (balance owed on monthly credit card statements)	_____
Installment Credit Contracts— remaining balance on following:	
Auto	_____
Furniture or appliances	_____
Mobile home	_____
Home improvement	_____
Other	_____
Cash loans (balance owed)	_____
Taxes due	_____
Income	_____
Property	_____
Loans against insurance policies	_____
Notes payable	_____
Total Liabilities	_____

*The equity in your home is considered an asset, which is why it is listed as such on this balance sheet. Practically speaking, unless you are willing to sell your home to pay for your daily expenses, you may consider taking it out of the equation for purposes of the exercise in Chapter Two.

Assets (What You Own That Has Value)

Liquid Assets _____
    Cash in your wallet _____
    Checking account _____
    Money market account _____

Savings Account _____
    Savings bonds _____
    Certificates of deposit _____
    Life insurance cash value _____

Securities (today's value) _____
    Stocks _____
    Mutual funds _____
    Bond certificates _____

Other Investments _____
    Annuities _____
    Tax shelters _____
    IRA/retirement _____

Personal Property (resale value) _____
    Car _____
    Motorcycle _____
    Bicycle _____
    Other vehicle _____
    Household furniture _____
    Antiques _____
    Furs, jewelry, silver _____
    Hobby equipment _____
    Art, collectibles _____

Loan Receivables Owed to You _____

Real Property _____
    Home/condo* _____
    Other _____

Total Assets _____

Total Assets _____

minus **Total Liabilities** _____

= **Total Net Worth** _____

Your total assets and liabilities should be reviewed annually to track your progress and gain an accurate understanding of your financial condition, if refining your priorities and goals should become necessary.

Financial Goals Should Track Priorities and Reality

The next step is to determine what your financial goals are. If you're like most up-and-coming professionals, the net worth calculation will reveal that your liabilities exceed your assets. If this is true, then your financial goals should include tackling that debt, as well as building the cash reserves and retirement nest egg. That's before you buy the BMW, Porsche, or the McMansion. Yes, you deserve these things, but believe this: five years from now, you will be better off, financially and emotionally, if you focus on paying off the debt, building your cash reserves, and establishing a retirement account before you spend to make yourself feel better. Indulgent spending will do little for your financial future and can cause undue stress and anxiety, if not now, certainly later. That being said, your age, health, family responsibilities, and lifestyle will all play a factor in determining what your financial wants and needs are. To help you get started, consider prioritizing the following:

_____ Paying off school debts	_____ Owning a car
_____ Paying off credit cards	_____ Owning a home
_____ Emergency savings account (equal to six months of paychecks)	_____ Retirement
	_____ Vacation
	_____ Children
_____ Insurance	_____ Elder care

This list is just a sampling of the common goals many professionals would consider relevant in their lives. You may have more, but this list is a starting point to prioritize what's important for you to accomplish over your income-producing years. Goals can be as short-term as buying a new suit next week, or mid-term, such as paying off credit card debt, or long-term with retirement. Here are age-appropriate goals for most young professionals to consider focusing upon:

20s	30s	40s
(1) Pay off Credit Cards, School, Car Debt	(1) Home Savings	(1) Investment
	(2) Domestic Life/Family	(2) Job Changes
(2) Establish Emergency Savings Fund	(3) Job Changes	(3) Family/ Elder Care
(3) Maximize Annual Retirement Contributions	(4) Continue to Max-out Annual Retirement Contributions	(4) Continue to Max-out Annual Retirement Contributions
		(5) Education-Child/Self

> Goals are personal, so decide what you want, as opposed to what someone wants for you. If you have a significant other or children, discuss your goals and priorities as a family. This discussion will be helpful later if your budget dictates that everyone make temporary or permanent sacrifices to achieve your family's financial goals.

Regardless of age, there are three general rules to follow while working to achieve your goals:

(1) Become and maintain a debt-free existence. There are many lenders who will always be willing to provide you with enough money for the lifestyle you want. However, they will charge a fee for this: a fee that can be better put to use in your savings account or funding one of your goals. Paying off debt, particularly consumer debt, is the best way to build wealth in the long run.

(2) Establish an emergency fund. An often ignored, yet crucial category is the emergency fund. You should have cash set aside equal to six months' pay. This is because the unexpected happens and often comes with a big price tag. If you don't have an emergency fund established for the curve-balls of life, you'll have to go (deeper) into debt. For example, car accidents with uninsured motorists, injuries in a softball game, family illness, or even being fired or laid off—all of these catastrophes commonly occur. You need a safety net so that when these unforeseen events happen, they don't thrust you into a deep (or deeper) financial hole.

(3) Max-out annual retirement contributions. Money set aside for retirement in a tax-deferred account is not taxed until retirement. Importantly, if your employer offers a retirement matching program, you should participate. By not participating, you're, in essence, giving up free money.

Once you've implemented these three rules, begin building your wealth by focusing on investments, as well as buying the homes, cars, clothes, and other accoutrements of wealth. Obviously, you must tailor these three rules to your particular situation. For example, if you have an emergency savings fund already established and no credit card debt, whether to enter the investment world (beyond the maximum retirement contribution) depends on the interest rate and manageability of the student loan debt. If the student loan debt (discussed in Chapter Three) is a manageable payment of $90, at an interest rate of 4 percent, it may be appropriate to consider investing (discussed in Chapter Seven) or saving for a home (discussed in Chapter Five) instead of an early pay-off of the student loan debt.

I Want That! Distinguishing between Want and Need

Distinguishing between a "want" and a "need" is critical to achieving your financial goals. You may want ten new power suits for your job, but you can get by with less, and with some employers, without any of them. Your monthly income and expenses will dictate whether to buy ten, five, or none, as discussed in Chapter Two.

Expectation versus Reality

When determining financial goals, set aside the expectations you may have had in school. Slogging over your studies, it's common to cook up big ideas with big outcomes, envisioning the fancy car, spiffy clothing, and sleekly furnished home you'll have when you finally graduate and begin your career. If you promised you'd reward yourself with a new BMW with that first paycheck, but you haven't paid off your debt, funded an emergency savings account, and maxed-out on your retirement contribution for the year, it's best for your financial reality to postpone the fulfillment of that promise. It doesn't necessarily mean you're unable to buy a car for transportation needs, just not a $50,000 model. Before caving into the expectations you had about the prospects of a lawyer's

Nicki graduated from the Ivy League straight to an elite law firm, debt-ridden, with $82,000 worth of student loans. Pampering her expensive tastes, and showing off her success with designer clothes, a modern apartment, and an expensive convertible was a reward for all her efforts and sacrifices made in seven years of school. Unfortunately, after two years of billing eighty-hour weeks, and concealing the dark circles under her eyes, she wanted out. After selling the car, getting a roommate, foregoing shopping sprees, she was still trapped in her job because of debt. She had to toil for another three-and-a-half years to pay it off. Securing a good financial footing paved her exit to a serendipitous job at a start-up.

life post-graduation (or other's expectations about what a lawyer's paycheck should get you or them), ask yourself this question: Am I willing to keep my legs pumping on the work treadmill for an extra five or ten years to indulge those expectations? For many, once they're actually on the job, the answer may be no.

Job Security

Priorities may fluctuate with the stability of your employment. Although you likely excelled in school, you may have yet to really prove yourself with your new employer. Not to place extra pressure on you or turn up the flames of competition for advancement or partnership, but one well-written memo on collateral estoppel is not proving yourself. You prove yourself by demonstrating value. It can take up to three years before you, as a worker, are truly profitable to your employer. Essentially, most lawyers learn the law (hopefully) in law school and spend the first four to five years of their career learning how to practice law, whether it's developing and trying a case, handling a merger or dealing favorably with clients. Until you have a day-to-day mastering of those skills, don't get too comfortable. This means some at your new employer may remain wary of you, and that translates to job insecurity. As a matter of fact, for many firms, it isn't until associates pass the five-year anniversary that a significant profit will actually have been made from the training that has been invested in them. (The five-year anniversary is also when many young lawyers can predict whether their future lies with the firm.)

Also, corporate bankruptcies and downsizing, law-firm mergers and rainmaking partners' exits can put even a go-to attorney's job in jeopardy. No matter how smart or skilled, if client work in a particular practice group dries up because of the economy, conflicts with a merging firm, or a partner's departure, an employer simply can't afford to keep an associate on when there is nothing to bill (no matter how profitable other areas in the firm are). Even plaintiffs' firms are not immune. Think about "King of Torts" Melvin Belli's firm filing for bankruptcy protection in 1995 after Dow Corning declared bankruptcy, leaving Belli with no way to recover the $5 million-plus he owed to experts and others who helped him in the suit he had won against Dow. For many young professionals, their employers will operate a treadmill paved with gold. Nevertheless, remain conscious of the potential for a slowdown; otherwise, your financial climb will become much more difficult without financial contingency preparation.

Sources and Resources

Kiplinger Magazine (April 6, 2007) ranked the following:

Best Overall Online Savings Account: HSBC Direct, *www.hsbcdirect.com*. (Annual percentage yield: 5.05 percent. Why it was the best: Quick customer service, an ATM card, a $1 minimum balance, online account with typically one of the highest yields.)

Chapter One

Simplest to Use: ING Direct, *www.ingdirect.com*. (Annual percentage yield: 4.50 percent. Why it was simplest: ING Direct's streamlined web site and four-step application are painless, offering online banking, no minimums, and no monthly fees.)

Best Online Checking Account: EverBank, *www.everbank.com*. (Annual percentage yield: Ranges from 3.25 percent for balances of less than $10,000 to 4.41 percent for $100,000 or more. Why it was the best: EverBank treats checking almost like savings. You need a minimum of $1,500 to open an account and enjoy an introductory rate of 6.01 percent for the first three months before it goes down to the market rate.)

Best Place to Vet Online Banks: Bankrate.com, *www.bankrate.com*. (Why it was the best: Interest rates and features change daily. This is a fast way to compare the full range of standard bank offerings as well.)

The Everything Personal Finance In Your 20's & 30's Book, by Debby Fowles (Adams Media 2004)

Ernst & Young's Personal Financial Planning Guide (5th ed., Wiley 2004)

The Only Other *Investment Guide You'll Ever Need*, by Andrew Tobias (Simon & Schuster 1987)

The "B" Word:
Everyone Needs a Budget

"The amount of money you have has got nothing *to do with what you earn. People earning a million dollars a year can have no money and people earning $35,000 a year can be quite well off. It's not what you earn, it's what you spend."*

Paul Clitheroe

A budget is your playbook for how you'll be spending and saving your money. It need not involve clipping coupons or austere measures. Rather, it helps to guide you toward your goals. Before you can prepare your plan for what you'll spend on and how much, you have to determine where your money has been going so that you can set realistic goals for your spending habits. If you haven't been keeping records of your spending and saving habits, now is the time to start. For the next month, record all checks, credit card charges, and ATM withdrawals to track your expenses. An organized recordkeeping system is a must for budgeting and financial success. Your recordkeeping can be as simple as putting pen to paper and creating a financial diary, or it can be computerized. The computer-generated recordkeepers are preferred by most because they also provide a financial analysis that summarizes expenses based on the information you key-in with a recommendation of the steps to take to achieve saving strategies. There are a number of software programs on the market, Quicken being one of the best-selling and user-friendly. It has several features you may never use, but is good for automatic reconciliation of bank statements, tracking expenses, budgeting, and gathering information for tax time. An important feature is that it allows you to print reports and easily compare what you're actually spending and saving with your budgeted financial goals.

Nevertheless, even if you purchase a computer program to track your finances, you ought to do a first draft of your own with a legal pad and pencil. Either way, when developing your plan, it's not important how it looks, just that the system works and you use it. It must be customized according to how you live.

Page One:
Add Up Your Annual Income

For most people, this is a short list consisting of your net monthly pay (after taxes are deducted from your paycheck). However, if you're fortunate to have additional income, such as a trust fund, dividends, or sales of paintings created in your spare time, list those, too. Do not include year-end bonuses or raises unless you have actually received them.

The purpose of this exercise is to determine what the average monthly income you have to allocate will be.

Page Two: Column A, List All Categories of Expenses

Rent, mortgage, gas, and charity are examples of the categories to include. In naming your categories, be as broad or specific as you want—whatever method works for you. For example, "Entertainment" can be all-encompassing, from dinners and DVD rentals to baseball tickets and bar-hopping, or you can list every specific event or activity as a subcategory of Entertainment. The important thing is that if you spend money on it, you list it. If you have a $20 co-pay for your semi-annual routine dental appointment, list it. Other annual expenditures such as auto insurance should also be listed, but calculate them on a monthly basis. For example, if your car insurance is $900 a year, divide it by twelve, and it is $75. If you own a car, include a category for maintenance costs. Similarly, if you own a condo or home, make sure to include a maintenance and repairs category. Though what may need fixing cannot always be anticipated, it is wise to set aside a certain amount per month. For example, if you've been told the roof will need replacing in four years, do not budget "zero" for the first three, and then $12,000 for the last year. Allocate $3,000 for each year and break it down even further to twelve monthly payments (of $250) to save for it.

Credit cards should not be listed as a category except the annual fee, if any. What you charge on the credit card, such as clothing, furniture, restaurants, and travel, are the cate-

gories to include on your list. As a guide, consider the sample
categories listed below.

Weekly Expenses	Monthly Expenses	Quarterly/ Annual Expenses
Food, Transportation	Rent/Mortgage, Utilities	Insurance, Taxes
Household Supplies	Phone, Loan Payments	Repairs, Clothing, Charity
Entertainment	Savings/ Investment	Pet Vaccinations, Licenses
Dry Cleaning	Medical/Dental/ Healthcare	Hair Stylist/ Barber

After listing all categories of expenses, take another stab
at it. Review the list and make certain there is nothing you
have left out: your afternoon Starbucks®, Friday Happy Hour,
iTunes downloads, pet toys, tailoring. Inevitably, there is likely something you have forgotten. Remember to include items
that are not always consistent, such as birthday and holiday
gifts, unreimbursed association fees, and the like. To get an
idea of what you spend, consider reviewing any records
(bills, credit card statements, receipts) you've kept from last
year. If you don't have records to recreate your expenses,
carry a notebook for the next month and jot down all of your
income and expenses, from gassing up your car to DVD
rentals. For the items that are yearly costs, divide by twelve
for an average monthly expenditure.

For ATM withdrawals, it's important to track where this

> **Taking Inventory:** If you're not a detail-oriented person or consider tracking every purchase too time-consuming and tedious, consider this for encouragement: one morning Starbucks® Venti adds up to $400 per year, a weekly bottle of wine can be $650 annually, and a pack-a-day cigarette habit, $1,700 per year. Assume you quit the habit and began investing the monthly cigarette money, at a 5 percent interest rate when you were twenty-five—by sixty-five, you'd earn over $325,000. Tracking all your expenses now will make it easier to figure out ways to make adjustments and save even more. Small amounts add up, so keep track!

cash goes, too. It can be time-consuming, but it is often the cash withdrawals that are most susceptible to slipping through your hands.

Next, analyze your monthly income and monthly expenses. If the total income figure is higher than expenses, you have a net positive cash flow that can be used, along with any funds you have already saved, to invest, buy a home, and further your goals. If your expenses are higher than income, however, you will need to reduce your expenses or increase your income to achieve a positive cash flow.

Page Two: Column B, Cost-Saving Adjustments

Once you've established how much you have available and where your money is going, the next step is to find ways to reduce spending and free up more cash for savings or putting toward your other goals. To the extent you have discretionary spending, this is usually the easiest category to start with. The idea is not one of deprivation but to channel money toward the goals that are important to you. For some, there may not be much fat in the budget to cut. It may become necessary to make lifestyle changes. For example, smoking is an expensive habit. If you've thought of quitting, now's the time to try and funnel that pack-a-day habit into a goal that is important to you. Do you have expensive hobbies, interests, or vices you can limit or eliminate? Ask yourself some tough questions about your lifestyle and interests, and how they mesh with your financial goals. Below are some tips for saving money to jump-start your brainstorming session.

Car and Maintenance

If you live in a city with readily available public transportation, ask yourself whether you can do without a car for a few years (and its gas, insurance, maintenance, and loan payment), or whether you can curtail its use and redirect the money you spend on gas to another goal. If you decide the cost of car ownership is worth the use or pleasure you receive from owning it, consider whether you can get by with a less expensive vehicle (for example, a BMW versus a Civic). If so, compare whether the profit from selling it and buying a cheaper model will help achieve your financial goals sooner.

Auto Insurance

Consider your deductible needs and weigh the likelihood of having an accident against paying for a higher deductible. Similarly, depending on the age of your vehicle, consider whether dropping collision coverage and retaining liability coverage is financially better for you. For example, a driver with a good driving record who owns a ten-year-old car may be financially better off with a $500 deductible instead of a $250 deductible, and dropping the collision coverage on a car that is likely worth only a few thousand dollars.

Housing

The general rule to follow is that housing costs should not exceed one-fourth of take-home pay; however, some regions (for example, New York City and San Francisco) can have sky-rocketing housing markets that make it difficult to follow this rule. If your rent is significantly higher because of the market you're in, consider whether to take on a roommate—even if only for a year—and put that rental income toward your financial goals. Utilities, telephone, cable, and Internet are common expenses whether you rent or own. If you own, remember to include property taxes in the mix. If the going gets really tough, consider whether you can live without cable, or lunches or dinners out for a while. Find ways to plug the drain on your paycheck—if not permanently, at least temporarily.

Phone Service

Make certain that your cellular phone service plan actually matches the minutes you use. Overpaying can add up. If you have a cellular phone and a land-line, consider whether you really need both. Also, if you decide to retain a land-line, long-distance carriers continually alter their plans. Consider reviewing whether you can save money with your long-distance carrier. Also, block international calling on your cell service—unless you need it—to deter fraudulent charges.

Entertainment

This is the category that is usually the easiest to target for cutbacks, though the items can be the most mentally difficult with which to part. Cover charges to bars and clubs, gourmet coffee drinks, movies, concerts, sporting events, poker night, art exhibitions, golf, subscriptions—if you can forego some of these activities for a while, financially you will have more to gain in furthering your goals. For example, spending 30 to 40 percent of your paycheck on entertainment is grossly out of line with your goals when you are nursing credit card debt.

Banking

Consider whether the fees, if any, you are paying for your accounts are really worth it. If you keep a low minimum balance in your checking account, consider switching to a bank with no minimum balance and no fees. If you're a debit card user, research banks that offer a "keep the change" program. In it, purchases are rounded up to the nearest dollar, and the difference can be deposited in your savings account.

Servicing Your Debt

Go over the list of everything you owe money on—car, student loans, credit cards, overdraft protection—and then determine what the interest rate is that you are paying on your loans, including credit cards, breaking down the principal and interest portion of your payments. Generally, if more than 36 percent of your income is servicing high-interest debts, you must schedule these in your goals for pay-off. Also, consider researching the credit cards offered by the organizations you have membership in. Some may offer a credit card with a lower interest rate (and lower annual fee). By the way, if paying off that debt is not one of your goals, reconsider with this fact in mind: paying interest is money that could be better directed to your own goals rather than making your lender rich. Chapters Three and Four will discuss, in detail, targeting student loan and credit card debts. For those who are used to spending more than they earn, this could become painful. If you start to crumble, just remember the interest portion of your payments could be funding financial goals that are important to you.

Classifieds and eBay

Are there unused items you have been storing for years (for example, clothes, furniture, musical instruments) that can be sold for cash?

Avoid Retail Therapy

Shopping for comfort or recreation is not conducive to accomplishing your financial goals. When you shop—

whether for groceries, clothes, electronics, single-malt Scotch, or a car—decide how much you have available to spend before you ever go online or step into the store. With a plan for spending, you should be questioning whether you really "need" that item. If you can achieve your financial goals without it, chances are you don't "need" it, you just "want" it. Don't deprive yourself of things you really need, but don't give in to impulse spending to make you momentarily feel good, either.

Gift Giving

Financial commitments to nonprofit or religious organizations, your alma mater, social service agencies or the arts, plus gifts at birthdays, weddings, baby showers, office celebrations, and holidays: it adds up. When creating a budget, allocate money for giving every month because you know you're going to need it. When the time to buy birthday or holiday presents actually arrives, it won't bust your budget. Consider picking up presents during sales year-round; last-minute shopping is when retailers can charge top-dollar. You need not be a Scrooge during the holidays, but you don't want to wake to a hangover when the partying is over, either. Overspending for most Americans occurs in December. Yet, just as you do for your own goals, make a list of people for whom you must purchase gifts and allocate a limit for each person, to stay on track.

These are only a few suggestions. Take the time to review your expenses in Column A, and consider what

"I'd be willing to take your pen and jab it into my eye if that would excuse me from sitting down and writing a budget," said Kent, a hard-working, highly paid, second-year associate, who had been lamenting that he never has enough money saved and can't get his credit cards paid off. His problem is not that he isn't earning enough, but that he doesn't know how to manage his money.

expenditures, if any, you can do without, and which ones can be tweaked for extra savings. The goal of this exercise is to develop information for a budget. The budget is going to be used to manage your cash flow so that you can pay your present expenses and still meet your life-long goals. You'll likely need to adjust your expenses to cover immediate needs and still achieve your short-term and long-term goals. Putting a temporary embargo on new purchases until the emergency savings account is built up is one example. Careful scrutiny of your personal habits and spending will likely identify more. Record all of them in Column B.

Many young professionals put off developing a budget until it's too late. Justifying the delay is easy to rationalize. For twenty-somethings (especially single twenty-somethings) the desire to enjoy the career that's just getting started is strong, including enjoying the fruits of hard work (cars, trips, clothing). When the thirties roll around, preoccupation with a mortgage and family responsibilities may begin. With the forties, an unexpected health crisis, medical expenses, family emergencies, as well as funding a child's college education fund may become the focus. Unfortunately, by the fifties, it's often too late to adjust expenses and accumulate significant savings for a comfortable retirement. With age comes wisdom, but youth also has an advantage: the earlier you start saving, the better for your financial future. Bottom line: Whatever your age, don't fall into the common trap of mortgaging your financial future to indulge a lifestyle. Before you wander down the path of rationalization, take control of your finances now. Bringing expenses under control may be easier than you think.

Page Three: The Budget

Now, it's time to create the actual budget. Analyze pages one and two and ask: Have I been living within my means? How much of my hard-earned money has gone to genuine needs and how much of the items could I have lived without? Distinguishing between what you "need" and what you "want" is critical to getting out of debt and building wealth. For example, people need food, shelter, and clothing. However, they may want perfume, cigarettes, football tickets, and new furniture. Many professionals find that they earn a decent income, are organized in their work life—and even their closets—but remain frustrated and vexed because they still can't seem to save enough or pay off their credit cards. Finding a higher-paying job is often not the solution, because they must fundamentally change how they handle their money. Even if a fantasy of winning thousands of dollars came true, it wouldn't help, because when income isn't properly allocated, it is spent, triggering a hike in living standards. A new suit, a bottle of single-malt Scotch for the poker buddies, a newer car, replacing the hand-me-down furniture with sleek new designs—it doesn't take long for a young professional to accumulate an even higher stack of bills.

Start with the bare necessities for your budget, then add on in accordance with allocating for your short-term and long-term goals. Begin the budget with these general guidelines:

(1) Max-out on Retirement Contributions. This is especially important if your employer has a matching program. Determine what the maximum contribution is for the year, and divide by twelve for the monthly amount to be deducted from your paycheck.

(2) Six Months' Cash Reserves. Build a safety net equal to six months' take-home pay to tackle any unexpected calamities, such as the loss of a job, medical expenses, or unexpected repair bills. The general rule is that the emergency fund should contain an amount equal to six months of your take-home pay. To estimate a monthly figure to include in your budget for emergency fund savings, try dividing six months of paychecks by twelve. Then, factor that amount into your monthly plan. Put the money in a money market fund or a short-term certificate of deposit to maximize your interest earnings.

(3) Savings. If you're maxing out on retirement contributions annually, and have a six months' cash reserve in place, consider whether to save more by investing, discussed in Chapter Seven. The general rule is to save 10 percent of your take-home pay. For some, that 10 percent may be usurped by maxing out on retirement contributions. However, for many, there may be nothing left over after all other expenses have been paid. This is when you need to carefully scrutinize where you can cut back—even if only temporary or periodically, such as redirecting the money you'd normally spend on weekend entertainment toward savings. Reducing the amounts you spend on discretionary or "want" items, can further your savings goals. Also, arrange for your paycheck to be automatically deposited to your checking account. It's the easiest way to build net worth because you are less tempted to spend it.

(4) Living Expenses. Allocate money for your rent or mortgage and property taxes, along with utilities.

(5) Food. Allocate money for your daily food needs.

(6) Transportation. Car payments, maintenance, gas, insurance, license and car registration, toll payments, and parking fees are legitimate expenses. For those without a car, include costs of public transportation.

(7) Healthcare. Premiums, co-pays, medication, dental fees, glasses, and contact lenses are all examples of unreimbursed expenses to budget for even if you have the best of employee benefit plans.

(8) Taxes. If taxes (federal, state, social security) are not taken from your paycheck, factor them in with your budgeting. (Then, you'd start with gross salary as your income, not take-home pay.)

(9) Children. While some expenses are necessary for child care, consider whether your child really needs another toy, designer outfit, or private lessons. Child care, babysitters, medicine, and diapers are all expenses that are necessary, and you need to include them in the budget.

(10) Vacation. Include vacations in your budget because, sooner or later, everyone needs a break, and there's a much greater chance for relaxation instead of anxiety if you've financially planned for the trip. Set a little aside on a monthly basis. If you're broke, consider less expensive travel, such as hiking or a biking trip with friends. Even if it's just taking a long weekend, sleeping in or staring at the wall, sipping martinis, remember to give yourself time to recharge.

Notice that savings-related concerns are the first items listed on the previous pages. Always pay yourself first—whether it's in the form of retirement contributions or a deposit to build the emergency fund—before you spend money on nonessential expenses. If you're in credit card debt, pay it off, but try to allocate money for your employer's matching retirement program, if any. Overall, it may not appear possible to pay yourself first, especially 10 percent of your monthly paycheck. Again, consider whether there are nonessentials that you are buying, and pay into savings what you can scrape together. If you can't handle missing the morning Starbucks® (or your co-workers can't handle your personality if you forego the morning Starbucks®), implement a savings progression system. Anytime you get coins back from a cash purchase, deposit them in a jar. At the end of the month, deposit the money into the emergency fund savings account. You can also do this with larger bills. When you receive change from a $5 bill, deposit the dollar bills and change into the jar, and at month's end into your emergency savings fund.

Implementing Your Budget

If you're new to budgeting, sticking to it may be difficult at first. If you fall off the wagon once in a while, don't beat yourself up (because there are plenty of people you'll meet in your career who'll try to do that for you, but don't let them beat you up either). Examine why you went off track. Learn from it and move one. Conversely, if you're repeatedly outspending what you earn, find another system that works for you. Sticking to a budget can be like sticking to a diet. If you deprive yourself, you'll develop uncontrollable cravings for things and eventually fail to stick to the plan. This means don't put down zero for "Entertainment" if you know you cannot live with it. A budget that doesn't leave money for an occasional, reasonably priced dinner out, or, when you have a family, an excursion together, will likely fail. Your budget is not meant to bind you to drudgery or a peasant's austerity.

Don't keep a lot of cash in your wallet. It's easier to splurge when cash is readily available to you. Direct deposit of paychecks and minimum cash withdrawals can help stop the hole in your safety net. Likewise, the most common slip-ups involve credit cards and recordkeeping. Remember, credit cards are not cash, especially when it comes to impulse spending. Regarding recordkeeping, it's important to keep track of the same expenses you did when preparing your budget. Good records will help you keep track of where

Chapter Two

Developing a Budget for Effective Financial Planning

1. Analyze Current Assets and Liabilities

2. Research Spending Habits, Actual Expenses, and Distinguish Needs from Wants

3. Determine Goals: Being Debt-Free, Saving for Emergency Protection, Accumulating Wealth, Minimizing Taxes, Preserving Wealth for Retirement

4. Draft Budget: Meet Present Daily Expenses and Short-, Mid-, and Life-Long Goals

5. Implement Budget and Periodic Review, Revise, and Update Budget as Necessary

---

your money comes from and where it goes. Computer software programs can help track expenses and provide reports and graphs to illustrate what you're spending your money on. A notebook, as well as keeping receipts for everything you buy, also works well. Another way to keep track is through your credit card statements, online banking or checking account statements. When you pay for purchases with checks or your credit card, you will have a monthly record of them. Also, remember to keep track of the items you purchase with cash. Whatever you do, use the system that works best for you.

At the end of each month, compare your actual expenses to your budget. Try to keep your spending within your plan, and look for ways to cut your expenses. Don't give up if maintaining your budget is hard for the first few months. It may take some time to set up a plan that works for you. Be flexible. If your budget is not working for you, fix it so it will. Computer software like Quicken can also help.

Finally, the budget need not be a well-honed document, but it should be thorough. Prevent napping at the financial helm by doing an annual check-up of your finances. Your budget will also require periodic updates or revisions to accommodate whatever event has occurred—pay raise, family responsibilities, unexpected debt or changes in the economy—that can affect your financial life.

In summary, the budget is the cornerstone of effective financial planning. It begins with analyzing your current assets and liabilities, identifying your "wants" and "needs," and then developing a plan for you to live by month-to-month in paying current expenses while laying out a strategy for achieving your life-long goals. It doesn't mean that you'll never be able to have your "wants," just that for some us, they have to be postponed. So, if you've been obsessing over the BMW or Porsche, stop tormenting yourself and give it a rest, at least until your debt is paid, emergency fund established, and retirement contributions are maxed out. Now, take this vision you've sketched for your finances, and apply the budget to your life.

Sources and Resources

www.intuit.com (Quicken software, also available at office supply stores and Amazon.com. Depending on the version purchased, priced around $30, after rebates.)

Inflation History and Predictions:

U.S. Department of Labor: *http://www.bls.gov*

Congressional Budget Office: *http://www.cbo.gov*

www.wife.org (Personal finance tips.)

www.stretcher.com (How to stretch a dollar.)

www.bls.gov (Bureau of Labor Statistics offers an *Occupational Outlook Handbook* that details salaries in different occupations.)

www.homefair.com (Offers a cost of living calculator for learning how much you'd need to earn to move to a new city in comparison with your current salary and city.)

"More Advice Graduates Don't Want to Hear," by Damon Darlin, *The New York Times*, June 2, 2007 (*www.nytimes.com*)

Budget Vacations:

www.priceline.com (Travel reservations and information such as 50 cities for $50 of less.)

www.lastminutetravel.com (Lists deals on the spur-of-the-moment for hotel and airfare.)

www.farecast.com (Shows cheap flights to major cities for travel in the next two weeks.)

www.site59.com (Sometimes can book just three hours prior to leaving.)

Student Loan Debt:
The Good, the Bad, and the Ugly

"Student loan debt collectors have power that would make a mobster envious."

Professor Elizabeth Warren,
Harvard Law School

Because student loans have a grace period on payment, they can seem like a sweetheart deal, but if you don't get a financial hold of things, they will leave a sour taste very quickly. If you graduated from a public law school, chances are you may be in a financial hole as much as $51,056 in student loan debt, $78,763 if you graduated from a private law school, according to student loan debt statistics maintained by the ABA Section of Legal Education and Admissions to the Bar. Add in any college student loans and the median lawyer's starting salary of $60,000 will not be enough to pay your "ambitions tax," the colloquial term coined for the financial price you have to pay for a graduate education these days. So, if you are a graduate whose student loan debt exceeds your starting salary—unless you have a benefactor to support you—you're going to have to learn to live with your student debt.

When it's time to begin making payments, your lender or servicer will establish a standard repayment schedule. (The model repayment plan establishes a minimum monthly payment amount of $50 with a maximum of ten years to repay the loan.) Contact your school's financial aid office if you are unsure who your lender is, or how to contact your lender. It may become important that you maintain contact with your lender over the life of your loan, especially if you experience a cash-crunch and difficulty in repayment. Similarly, if you have moved, provide your lender with current address information so that it can provide you with the loan payment materials. The day after you graduate, withdraw, or drop to less than half-time status, the six-month grace period begins. Expect your first loan payment to be due thirty to forty-five days after the end of the grace period. For debt-ridden young professionals, there are repayment options such as consolidation, loan deferment, and forbearance. Each has unique advantages, disadvantages and eligibility requirements, as discussed below.

Student Loan Consolidation

Loan consolidation is for those with multiple loans, with different lenders, requiring you to write more than one check for monthly payment. Loan consolidation enables you to bundle all your loans into a single loan with one lender and one repayment plan. By consolidation, the balances of your existing student loans are paid off, with the total balance rolling over into one consolidated loan. The result is that you have only one loan to pay. Both students and their parents can consolidate loans.

The benefits of loan consolidation are that it: (1) locks-in a fixed, possibly lower rate,[1] for the term of your loan; (2) lowers your monthly payment; (3) combines everything into one monthly payment. In addition, consolidated loans should have no fees, charges, or prepayment penalties, and may offer flexible repayment options. Obviously, you should consider consolidating your loans if the consolidation loan would have a lower interest rate than your current loans. Student loan providers such as Sallie Mae have proclaimed that consolidating student loans can reduce monthly payments by up to 54 percent. However, the only way to reduce your payment this much is to extend your repayment plan. Typically, you have ten years to repay student loans. Depending on the amount you're consolidating, extending the repayment plan up to thirty years may be possible; however, the longer it takes to repay the loan, the more interest you're paying. It comes down to what amount you can manage to pay on a monthly basis while still remaining true to your long-term financial goals. On the positive side, there are no prepayment penalties, so if you choose to extend the payments beyond ten years, you can always pay off the loan early. The negative

---

1. While the interest rate for Stafford loans made after July 1, 2006, is fixed, loans prior to that date were made at a variable interest rate tracking the July 1 Treasury bills.

is that, for some borrowers, the only way to obtain the lowest interest rate is to extend the time period of the repayment of the loan, which may result in more interest being paid. Also, if you are close to paying off your existing loans, consolidation may not offer you any savings.

The interest rate for the consolidated loan will be calculated by averaging the interest rate of all the loans being consolidated, and then rounding up to the next one-eighth of 1 percent. The maximum interest rate is 8.25 percent. You can calculate your interest rate by visiting *www.salliemae.com* or *loanconsolidation.ed.gov* for an online calculator.

Whether loans qualify for consolidation depends upon the following criteria: (1) you are in your six-month grace period following graduation or you have started repaying your loans; (2) you have eligible loans totaling over $7,500; (3) you have more than one lender; (4) you have not already consolidated your student loans, or, since consolidation, you have gone back to school and acquired new student loans. Most loans are eligible for consolidation. To begin the consolidation process, check with the lenders that hold your current loans. It may be possible to consolidate through any bank or credit union that participates in the Federal Family Education Loan Program, or directly from the U.S. Department of Education. Generally, the loan terms and conditions will be the same, regardless of where you consolidate. However, if all your loans are with one lender, you must consolidate with that lender.

You can only consolidate once, unless you go back to school and take out more loans. This means that you should research and make certain that you have found the best deal possible. While the interest rate may be the same from all lenders, you may find some lenders willing to provide future rate discounts for prompt payment, as well as a discount for having monthly payments directly debited from your checking account. If you are married, it is permissible for a married couple to consolidate loans but not advisable. This is because both of you will always be responsible to repay the loan, even if you later separate or divorce. Also, should you need to defer payment on the loan, both of you will have to meet the deferment criteria.

Regarding the time frame for consolidation, while you can consolidate your loans any time during your six-month grace period or after you have started repaying your loans, you have a better chance at getting the lowest rate if you consolidate during your grace period. Practically speaking, because you will lose the rest of the grace period, it is recommended that consolidation occur near the fifth month of the grace period. The consolidation process usually takes thirty to forty-five days. With respect to private loans (non-government guaranteed loans), the interest rates and fees are usually higher than for government-backed loans such as federal Stafford loans. Thus, consolidation should lock-in a lower interest rate and save money for those graduates carrying private student debt. Graduates who consolidate during the grace period—the six months before you are required to begin monthly payments—could lock in a low rate around 4 percent.

Consolidation is not available if you are still in school.

A new mother, Margaret, began her career with a starting salary of $145,000, with $200,000 in college and graduate student debt. The interest for $56,000 in private debt was 9.2 percent, for which she obtained a one-year forbearance on payment. She consolidated the remaining government-backed debt for a manageable 4 percent rate.

Another disadvantage to consolidation is that you may have to waive certain defenses. So, if you anticipate challenging the loan in court, certain arguments may be barred. Some financial experts advise that the older your loan, the better chance you have to negotiate a settlement with the lender on payment for a reduced amount, so it would be best not to consolidate old loans. As a practical matter, this doesn't work for most graduates, because to settle for a significantly reduced amount that would save you more money than consolidation, lenders usually require a lump-sum cash payment of a major portion of the loan, and most graduates cannot afford the lump-sum payment.

Finally, the decision to consolidate should not be automatic. If a lower interest rate is your goal, some lenders offer a discount for on-time payments (forty-eight-consecutive on-time loan payments) of up to two percentage points. Research what makes financial sense for you before you act. The online calculators, mentioned previously, can run computations.

Student Loan Deferment

A student loan deferment allows you some flexibility in repaying your student loans as long as you meet certain criteria. The primary benefit of deferment is that the payment and accrual of interest is suspended. Lenders typically extend a deferment for up to three years. In order for you to apply for deferment based on your economic situation, most lenders will require you to apply every year and prove why you deserve to have your repayment suspended. Eligibility requirements may vary by lender, but the most common are summarized as follows:

Pregnancy or Adoption and Caring for a Newborn

If you are not working, no longer in school, and have attended school within the last six months for at least half-time, you may qualify for this student loan deferment. Proof, such as a doctor's statement or records, a copy of the birth certificate or statement from the adoption agency referencing placement, will be required. Certification from your school concerning your enrollment status may also be required. The deferment has a maximum time limit of six months. If you are unable to start repaying your student loans when the deferment expires, you may seek another type of loan deferment.

Economic Hardship

The way this works is, you need to have income below the "standard of living" as determined by the U.S. Bureau of Statistics. Keep in mind you may need to provide proof in this situation. For many, obtaining deferment because of economic hardship is difficult because you must be able to affirm that your monthly income does not exceed the larger of the federal minimum wage rate or the poverty line for a family of two (regardless of the your actual family size). The lender will have worksheets to help you determine whether you satisfy these criteria.

Active Duty

Borrowers in the U.S. military, National Oceanic and Atmospheric Administration (NOAA), U.S. National Guard in time of war or state of emergency, or officers in the commissioned corps of the U.S. Public Health Service may qualify for deferment.

Disability

If, unfortunately, you become disabled and unable to work for more than sixty days, or you need to care for a disabled spouse or dependent for more than ninety days, then you may be eligible for deferment. To the extent you are totally and permanently disabled, federal student loans can be discharged, but not private student loans, absent a bankruptcy filing, which still requires a threshold showing of hardship.

Unemployment

You'll need to be working less than thirty hours per week or in a job that is not expected to last more than ninety days. You will likely also be asked to substantiate this with proof, so it's wise to keep records about your job search efforts and

Chapter Three

> John's starting salary was $75,000, with $92,000 in student debt. Because he had to relocate due to a hurricane, he negotiated a one-year forbearance. He then consolidated his loans to a more manageable 4 percent interest rate.

documentation from any unemployment benefits. In most cases, an unemployment verification will be done to confirm your status.

Parental Leave

Borrowers who have pre-school-age children, and are entering or re-entering the work force may qualify for a deferment. Federal PLUS loans are not eligible. The maximum cumulative time frame allowed for the deferment is twelve months.

Submit a deferment request directly to your lender. Most lenders offer forms online, so you can apply for a deferment by downloading the appropriate form, completing and signing it, then sending to the loan holder. Unless you receive notice that your deferment request has been approved, the loan payment due dates remain in place. Check with your lender or the company that services the loan for more information about processing. In general, deferments cost lenders money because they are not accruing interest on the debt. Thus, though a lender may initially be reluctant to discuss this option, a debt-ridden graduate should still inquire.

Loan Forbearance

Student loan forbearance is a worthwhile option to consider when you find yourself ineligible for student loan deferment. Student loan forbearance is granted at the discretion of the lender. Lenders usually grant forbearance if you are in poor health or experiencing other personal problems. Lenders must grant forbearance when your Title IV student loan debt equals or exceeds 20 percent of your gross income and you submit a written request. Under those circumstances, a lender must grant forbearance for one year, and shall renew it for a second and third year under certain conditions. Moreover, the fact that you are granted a forbearance cannot be the cause of a negative credit report and no fees can be charged. Unfortunately, this right is limited to loans held by lenders. It does not apply if the loan has been taken over by a guaranty agency or the Department of Education.

Generally, approval of a loan forbearance request is easier to get than a payment deferment request. However, the downside of forbearance is that the interest continues to accrue, even though the loan payments are reduced or postponed. The positive is that forbearance could allow you to avoid default during the time in which you are unable to afford to make payments. Once granted, a forbearance allows for a temporary postponement of student loan payments, extension of the repayment schedule and may also allow for reduced loan payments. Though there are four types of forbearance, the two types that you can request from a lender are discretionary forbearance and mandatory forbearance, as summarized below. (The other two types, administrative and mandatory administrative, are mainly used by the lender to apply to certain situations.)

You may be granted discretionary student loan forbearance when you can demonstrate that certain financial hardship situations exist that impact the repayment of your debt. Common situations that may qualify are: (a) in school with an enrollment status of less than half-time. (Remember, if your status is more than half-time you may qualify for student loan deferment); (b) unemployed (when you have surpassed the maximum deferment time limit); (c) poor health; (d) working fewer hours through a reduction of hours by your employer; (e) experiencing a sudden life circumstance that impacts your income, such as the community in which you live being designated a disaster area. Discretionary forbearance can also take the form of reduced payments. The benefit of reducing the monthly payment amount is that it may be more manageable for you.

Most people will not qualify for mandatory forbearance because of the specialized categories of eligibility, which include: (a) you are participating in an internship or residency program (beyond the time-frame requirements for a deferment); (b) you are in a national service position where the National and Community Service Trust Act of 1993 applies; (c) you fall under the Teacher Loan Forgiveness Program; (d) you are participating in a qualifying service as defined by the Child Care Provider Loan Forgiveness Program; or (e) you are participating in qualifying service for partial loan repayment under the Student Loan Repayment Programs administered by the U.S. Department of Defense.

Interest is the primary difference between forbearance and deferment. You will always be responsible for all interest that accrues during the period of forbearance. During a deferment, you will be responsible for the interest that accrues if your loans are unsubsidized Stafford loans. If you have subsidized Stafford loans, you will not be responsible for the interest that accrues during a deferment. You can pay the interest during a period of forbearance or deferment— definitely the cheaper route in the long run—otherwise, your lender may capitalize the interest at the end of the forbearance or deferment period. When interest is capitalized, it will increase the amount of interest you have to pay.

A final point to consider is that forbearance may not automatically lock-in the lowest interest rates. If you are carrying private student debt and locking in a lower interest rate is your primary concern, student loan consolidation should be pursued first, or in conjunction with forbearance.

Alternative Repayment Plans

Other than the standard loan payment schedule of paying the minimum payment set by your lender over ten years or less, your lender may offer other types of repayment schedules. Some plans may result in more interest being paid over the life of the loan, however. Such plans include:

Graduated Repayment

Under this plan, monthly payments will gradually increase during your repayment period. The early payments are lower, which is both a positive and a negative. It is negative because

Alisha, a legal-aid lawyer, placed her loans in forbearance twice since graduating in 2001. Because of the accrual of interest, the loan balance increased from $21,000 to $28,000. After consolidating her loans, her monthly payment is $175 instead of $325, allowing room in her budget to fully participate in her employer's matching retirement plan.

it includes mostly interest so you don't pay the balance quickly and pay more interest. On the positive side, the manageability of the monthly payment is appealing because it anticipates that, as you advance in your career, you'll earn more money to make the larger payment.

Income-Sensitive or Income-Contingent Repayment

Here, monthly payments will be based on the amount of money you earn. Between 4 percent and 25 percent of your gross income each month is paid over a fifteen-year period, or a twenty-five-year period on the contingent plan.

Extended Repayment

This plan is similar to the income-sensitive or income-contingent, except that it usually applies to borrowers with debts in excess of $30,000 of federal student loans.

Finally, you always have the option of pre-payment, at any time, on all or a portion of the balance owed on your loan without penalty. A combination of approaches may best satisfy your needs. This is why contacting your lender to research and review your options is necessary for before you act.

Loan Repayment Assistance Program

Lawyers in public-interest law may find that their state offers a loan repayment assistance program by way of grants or loan forgiveness. Eligibility for these programs varies greatly. Also, graduates should ask whether their law school offers a loan payment assistance program. Often, law schools have easier eligibility requirements than those of the state governments.

Loan Forgiveness Program

The government limits the loan forgiveness program to certain teaching and childcare providers, nursing, and military positions. Thus, most graduates do not qualify for this program.

Late Payments

Late student loan payments are reported to credit reporting bureaus. This information may stay on your credit history for up to ten years—unless you rehabilitate the loan—and be considered by other lenders when you purchase a car, home, and seek credit for other things.

Loan Default

Despite the accumulation of interest, loan forbearance is a better alternative to default. For federally guaranteed student loans under Title IV of the Higher Education Act, default occurs when you fail to make payments on your loan for (a) 180 days if you repay in monthly installments or (b) 240 days if the payments are due less frequently. The lender must exercise "due diligence" during the time that you are behind in your payments. Due diligence involves the lender's making repeated efforts to find you and contact you about repayment. Ultimately, the lenders will turn the loan over for collection to the U.S. Department of Education or the guaranty agency in your state. Lenders may accelerate a defaulted loan, which means that the entire balance becomes due in a single payment. The collection fees can be added to the loan for payment. A default will also be reported to credit bureaus, and your credit rating may suffer because it will show up in the negative on a credit report. Worse, the government is permitted to seize a borrower's tax refunds, garnish wages, and withhold federal benefits such as social security, if a loan is in default. Once a loan has been declared in default, it is no longer entitled to a deferment or eligible for forbearance. You can also be denied any further student aid should you pursue additional studies. Consequently, before allowing the loan to default, contact your lender to try to work something out. Most lenders would rather have a loan voluntarily paid than turn it over to collection. The key is not waiting until the last minute. Take affirmative steps to contact your lender and discuss the options that are available to you if you find yourself financially strapped.

Loan Rehabilitation Program

Sometimes a defaulted loan may be reinstated by the Department of Education under its loan rehabilitation program. Typically, this requires twelve consecutive monthly payments, though you can also pay off your entire student debt in one lump sum. When you enter into a repayment agreement with your lender, guaranty agency, or collection agent, a new loan is created that wipes out the defaulted loan. The benefit of loan rehabilitation is that, once a loan has been rehabilitated, it will be taken out of default and the credit bureau reports made by the servicing agency will be deleted. You will be able to repay the loan, usually over a nine-year period, and regain eligibility for additional Title IV student financial aid funding if you pursue further studies.

Bankruptcy

If your obligation to repay a student loan is discharged in bankruptcy, any co-signers or endorsers of your debt are not discharged. For example, if your parents co-signed your student loan, they are still liable for repayment. Bankruptcy may not be your best option, however, because borrowers have an incredibly high burden of proof. To discharge student loan debt in bankruptcy, borrowers must essentially prove that they will fail to maintain a minimal standard of living if they were forced to repay, and that such failure will continue into the foreseeable future. For a lawyer, filing personal bankruptcy is the equivalent of career suicide. To achieve discharge of the student loans, you're basically going to have to argue that you're never going to have a sustainable career.

While in the 1970s, young professionals filing bankruptcy to rid themselves of student loan debt was commonplace, congressional amendments to the bankruptcy code have made the task more difficult. Courts will likely consider practical considerations, such as whether the borrower can find a higher-paying job, has done everything possible to try to cut the payments to a manageable amount, and what types of efforts were made, if any, to attempt repayment before deciding to file bankruptcy. Any grace periods, forbearances, or deferments must be subtracted from the time elapsed between when the first payment became due and the bankruptcy filing date, which can also be critical in calculating whether the debt will be discharged. In any event, before choosing bankruptcy as an option, it is strongly recommended that you investigate the other options detailed here, and discuss those options with your lender.

Errors with Student Loans

Errors in recordkeeping, such as payments not being credited properly, incorrect interest rates assigned, and incorrect personal information, commonly occur. When you discover an error in your student loan, contact your lender immediately. If you are unable to resolve it, contact the Federal Student Aid Ombudsman of the Department of Education at 1-877-557-2575. You may be able to manage your student loans online at *www.manageyourloans.com*, which allows you to view the status of your loan, make payments, correct or update contact information, and, in some instances, change your payment plan.

Tax Deductions

Subject to satisfying certain criteria, the interest you pay on your student loans may be deductible. Eligibility depends on your income level, and whether the proceeds of your loans were used to fund qualified higher-education expenses (tuition, fees, room and board, school supplies). If you paid more than $600 in interest on your student debt during the year, the lender should send you a Form 1098-E, showing the amount paid. In order to claim this amount on your income taxes, a Form 1040 or 1040A must be filed. Unlike mortgage interest, you do not have to itemize deductions to take advantage of this deduction.

Strategy for Managing Student Debt

Balance your immediate need for a low monthly payment with your long-term financial goals. While lenders work within the confines of the promissory note, they'd rather find a way to achieve voluntary payment of the loan than involuntary, so make it work for you. The goals for student debt are to get the interest rate as low as possible within the shortest time frame to pay it off. If that doesn't give you a manageable monthly payment and there are no other ways to cut back on your living expenses, then go for a longer payment plan, because there should be no early pay-off penalties if circumstances change and you are able to pay the debt off sooner than anticipated. It is wise to include your student loan debt in the periodic review of your finances to ensure that you have obtained the most favorable terms possible for your

Chapter Three

financial situation. The key to remember in managing your student loan debt is that, until you contact your lender about options that may be available to you, it is unlikely your situation will improve.

Sources and Resources

For additional information regarding student loans, check the following web sites:

U.S. Department of Education Debt Collection Service: Guide to Defaulted Student Loans
http://www.ed.gov/offices/OSFAP/DCS

William D. Ford Federal Direct Loan Program Home:
http://www.ed.gov/offices/OSFAP/DirectLoan

National Consumer Law Center:
http://www.consumerlaw.org

U.S. Department of Education Debt Collection Service: Guide to Defaulted Student Loans:
http://www.ed.gov/offices/OSFAP/DCS

Bankruptcy: For a factual pattern where the appellate court affirmed the bankruptcy court's discharge of student loans, see *In Re: Jeri Lynn Lee, Debtor. Jeri Lynn Lee, Plaintiff-Appellees v. Regions Bank Student Loans; Defendant-Appellant*, Case 06-6049 (8th BAP 9/26/06); Compare *Rose v. U.S. Dep't of Ed. (In re Rose)*, 187 F. 926 (8th Cir. 1999).

www.irs.gov (Topic 456—Student Loan Interest Deduction)

Credit:
How to Use It Wisely

"Credit buying is much like being drunk.
The buzz happens immediately and gives you
a lift . . . the hangover comes the day after."

Dr. Joyce Brothers

For corporate types who understand how to structure business deals using debt as a tool for profit, seeing debt as the enemy in one's personal life can be difficult. However, the overall principle is the same: shrewdly managing debt in your overall financial structure can save you money. If you're using only one, low-interest credit card, vigilantly paying off the balance every month so you accrue no interest or finance charges, you need read only the credit report section of this Chapter. But if you're carrying a monthly balance on one or multiple credit cards with varying interest rates, been denied credit or had a credit card rejected, read on.

Credit Cards

Credit card use can overthrow, if not collapse, a healthy financial structure. Worse than being a slave to your paycheck is being dependent on the available balance of your credit card. If you are like many graduates, you used a credit card to help bridge the gap in your finances during school. According to a survey conducted by student lender Nellie Mae, grads leave school with an average credit card balance of $2,169, and may hold up to four credit cards with interest rates varying from 13.7 percent to 18 percent. Starting today, going forward, credit cards as a means of borrowing should be your second-to-last resort—the pawn and cash advance shops that charge more than 24 percent being the last resort. Why? Because a key component to financial success is paying off your credit cards. Truly, the simplest way to earn extra money, tax-free and risk-free, is to pay off your credit cards. If you're not forced to pay 18 percent interest, it's akin to earning 18 percent. The minimum monthly payment for most credit cards is about 2 percent of the balance, including interest. When you don't pay off your credit card each month, you're actually paying an inflated price for your purchases, while increasing the credit card company's profits.

> The purchase of a $2,500 chair at an annual interest rate of 18 percent takes 28 minimum monthly payments to pay off the balance. That's $5,896 in interest for the credit card company, bringing the real cost of the chair to $8,396, not to mention the lost savings and interest that could have been earned for you on the $5,896. In contrast, if you were able to redirect that minimum payment for thirty years into a monthly $50 deposit to an 8 percent account, you'd earn over $62,000.

Translation: Pay Off the Credit Cards!! The intelligent way to use credit cards is to:

(1) Pay off the balance every month. When you pay off the monthly balance within the grace period, credit cards become an interest-free convenience. Be extra careful about paying within the grace period. Pay electronically, if possible, or mail the payment well within the deadline to avoid late-payment accruals, because some cards can take up to seven working days to process a payment.

(2) Research credit cards. Select a card (American Express, Discovery, MasterCard, Visa) that offers you the lowest interest rate, low annual fee, no or limited finance charges. Cash-back or travel award programs may offer higher interest rates, so research what you're actually getting in exchange for paying for the privilege. Earning frequent flier miles is not a good reason to choose one card over another unless everything else is equal.

(3) Use only one personal credit card. (If your employer provides you with a business card, obviously, only use the business card for authorized business use.) This practice reduces the urge to splurge, and limits the number of calls you have to make if it gets lost or stolen. (Federal law provides that the most you will owe for unauthorized charges is $50 per card if you are unable to report your card lost or stolen before a thief uses it).

(4) Avoid cash advances. Those convenient checks occasionally delivered in the mail with your statement are not checks. They are worse than using your credit card because there is no grace period. The minute you cash the so-called check, interest starts running. There may also be a transaction fee of up to 3 percent of the cash advance total.

(5) Invest in a shredder. Destroy all discarded receipts, credit card statements (not being saved for tax purposes discussed in Chapter Eight) and even credit card solicitations to prevent identity theft.

(6) Review billing statements every month. Confirm that the transactions made on your account were purchases or charges you authorized. (You have sixty days to notify the credit card company in writing, with the company having thirty days to respond and ninety days to resolve or correct the error. You're not required to pay the disputed amount and should not incur any finance charges on the disputed amount while the company is investigating the matter).

Digging Out of Debt

All right, so you're on board with paying off the credit cards, but how do you do it? When you're running on empty, paying off credits cards is easier said than done. If you've reached the point where you accept the fact that you've accumulated too much credit-card debt, follow these steps. Step 1: pledge that you'll change the way you use credit cards to avoid falling back into the same financial hole. Step 2: store all credit cards in a safe, secure location where they won't get lost or stolen, and you won't be tempted to use them. Step 3: develop a plan to pay down the debt by considering the suggestions listed below, as well as reviewing the cost-cutting measures outlined in Chapter Two on budget preparation.

Stop Using Credit Cards

Stop using your credit cards, and especially avoid retail store and gas station cards. If you slip and sneak a credit card quickie, destroy the credit cards. If you don't trust yourself, destroy them now. Regarding retail cards, close the accounts once they are paid off. The closing of the account may affect your overall credit score, discussed below. Closing them eliminates overspending and reduces identity theft opportunities.

Cash-In

The highest rate of return on your savings account is likely to be lower than the interest payment due on your credit cards. If you have savings, consider cashing it in to pay off the credit cards. Optimally, leave at least three months worth of no-frills living expenses in the account. Another option is to borrow against any life insurance policies. If you pass away before the balance of the loan is paid, the margin plus the interest can be deducted from any settlement that is due to your beneficiary.

Home Equity Loan

If you own your home, you could qualify for a home equity loan that can move you from 18 percent interest payments to around 7 percent. Essentially, you're using your home as another credit card. The advantage is that, if you itemize your deductions, at tax time, a portion of the interest may be deductible. Once the home equity proceeds pay off your credit card, do not use the credit card or incur more debt until you have paid off the home equity loan. The mechanics of home equity loans are discussed in further detail below. For now, know that a home equity loan should be viewed only as a one-time bail-out method for your high-interest consumer debt. Do not use it to transform your home into an ATM.

Refinancing

If you haven't damaged your credit rating yet, refinancing may allow you to collapse your debts and roll them into a new mortgage. When interest rates are lower than the current mortgage rate, this option may make sense for you. Refinancing is discussed further in Chapter Five.

Borrowing from Retirement

Most 401(k) plans allow you to borrow up to 50 percent, or $50,000, whichever is smaller. The downsides are: (1) you will be paying back the loan with after-tax money and the interest will be taxed again when you finally cash out the account at retirement; and (2) it will detour your savings progress. However, the interest rate will be cheaper than the interest paid on the credit card. If you quit or lose your job, the debt becomes due immediately. If you should be unable to pay it, the amount outstanding will be treated as a distribution. This means you'll receive a tax bill, including a penalty if you're under 59-1/2. Obviously, the best way to avoid the tax bill is to ensure that the loan is paid off before you change jobs.

Research Best Card and Transfer Balances

Lawyers love fine print in practice, but surprisingly few actually read it in their personal transactions. Read the fine print of your credit card contract. If you have more than one credit card, make certain the balance owed is the highest on the card with the lowest interest rate. Research whether there are costs associated with transferring balances to the lowest interest rate card. A 1 percent transfer fee or $50 is common, and, when you transfer several cards, that adds up, so calculate over time whether the fees are worth it in comparison to the amount of interest you'd be paying. Be cautious of unsolicited credit offers. Mail solicitations often pronounce a fantastically low interest rate effective during the promotional period. Before credit card hopping, ask what the interest rate will be when the promotional period ends, as well as the date the promotional period ends. Obviously, if you're switching cards, the new rate should not be higher than the one you're switching from. Some offers only apply the low interest rate if the balances have been kept for twelve months, or if the balance is paid off within the promotional period. Finally, some introductory offers carry a penalty for transferring the debt to another card when the promotional period of low interest is over—another reason to ask questions and read the fine print. Transferring balances and closing accounts may negatively affect your credit scores, but if you're swimming in debt, the first goal is to get rid of it. There are better ways to improve your credit than continuing to keep high-interest accounts open that you will be too tempted to use.

Renegotiate Terms with the Credit Card Companies

When you've exhausted all alternatives, including nothing to sell or cash-in, contact your creditors and renegotiate a new, lower repayment schedule. Possible arguments include beginning with research concerning other credit cards for their interest rates and asking whether your company can match the deal to keep you as a customer, to simply explaining you can't afford to pay and learn what the company, if anything, can do for you on a lower repayment schedule. It should be mentioned that there are organizations that specialize in guiding people out of debt. The "debt doctors" will contact your creditors and try to negotiate lower monthly payment requirements and interest rates. But be aware that you also incur a monthly fee for these services. As an educated professional, consider making the time to contact your credit card companies yourself, especially if this is the first time you've gotten into serious financial trouble.

Borrowing from a Relative or Friend

If you're not proud, or if you are and can swallow your pride long enough to ask a relative or friend for a loan, consider this option. As all lawyers know, be sure to document the loan with a written agreement detailing a schedule for repayment and interest rate. From an interpersonal perspective, if you choose this option, choose your source wisely, as there may be psychological ramifications to your relationship, unless you borrow from a pessimist, as Groucho Marx joked, because they never expect to be repaid.

Personal Bankruptcy Is the Last Resort

Besides the legal fees, and ten-year stain on your credit record, a personal bankruptcy filing will not likely help a lawyer's career. Proceed with this option using extreme caution and only as a last resort. Your second-to-last resort is talking to your creditors to see if you can work something out. Some creditors may allow you an extra couple of months to catch up on debt, in exchange for tacking on missed payments at the end of the loan. Nevertheless, if your negotiations fail, there are two types of personal bankruptcy relief: Chapter 7 and 13. Chapter 7 allows the discharge of most debts except for alimony, child support, taxes, loans obtained through filing false financial statements, loans not listed in the bankruptcy petition, legal judgments against the petitioner, and student loans. Chapter 13 allows for a wage-earner plan where you may keep most of your property under a court-approved repayment plan based on your resources that pays off all or part of your debt over a three- to five-year period. The benefits of a bankruptcy filing are that any creditor harassment must stop when you file, and, under Chapter 13, when all provisions of the court-approved plan are met, you emerge debt-free.

Avoid the Minimum

What do we think of people who only do the minimum? The line from the movie *Office Space* applies to credit cards. Never do the minimum. Though you may not be able to pay it off, scrape together every penny that you can, and pay as much as you can above the minimum payment. The more you pay down every month, the faster that debt disappears, sometimes years sooner. For example, consider the next chart, which illustrates a $20 minimum payment on a $1,000 debt versus adding an extra $20 a month and paying $40.

	Interest Rate	Months to Pay	Total Payments
$20/month	6%	56	$1,126.97
	12%	67	$1,353.43
	18%	89	$1,783.97
For an extra $20…			
	Interest Rate	Months to Pay	Total Payments
$40/month	6%	25	$1,025.24
	12%	27	$1,103.28
	18%	29	$1,199.00

Deter Solicitations

Contact one of the three U.S. credit bureaus and request removal from all prescreened credit offer lists. Those credit bureaus are Equifax, Experian, and Trans Union. Limiting solicitations also limits the risk of identity theft. Identity thieves commonly intercept solicitations, substituting their own name and address, then max-out the card before you know what's happening.

Exercise Patience

Impatience often leads to borrowing money to buy things that quickly depreciate and lose value, such as cars, clothing, and furniture. Consequently, you pay much more for the item than the price tag when the interest on the credit card or

If you don't think your credit-card use is a problem, ask yourself whether you: (1) are living paycheck to paycheck and have little or no savings; (2) have more than two credit cards and only pay the minimum balance; (3) were denied credit or had your credit card rejected; (4) compulsively buy things you don't need or use when you shop; (5) use cash advances to pay bills. A "Yes" answer suggests that credit-card use is likely at a financially dangerous level. Remember, there's no quick fix to carrying too much debt, except to stop the spending habits that brought the debt about in the first place.

other loan is added. If you can't afford it, don't charge it. Wait, save, and then buy when you can pay cash, or can pay off the charge (and total balance) when the item appears on your credit-card statement.

Once the credit cards are paid off, before you use credit again, consider what kind of spender you are. Take the "Spender Quiz" in the Appendix and you may learn more about your money attitudes and habits.

Financing a Car

Don't. If you can afford to pay cash, do it. The exception to the rule is 0 percent financing when it's coupled with a reasonable sales price. In fact, when dealers advertise interest rates on sale, a good shot at getting a good price is to inform the dealer you'll be paying cash.

However, because not everyone can afford to pay cash for a BMW or Porsche and 0 percent isn't usually available, young professionals should consider purchasing a less expensive new car or a gently pre-owned (used) car. The overall savings isn't just the purchase price, but insurance, maintenance, operating costs, and financing. If the savings of purchasing a compact or pre-owned car equaled a $10,000 bonus in your pocket, would you still care about whether your colleagues will be impressed when you park something fancier in the office garage? (The financially healthy answer to that question—if you don't have your credit cards and student loans paid off, and an emergency savings fund established, and are financially unable to max-out your annual retirement contribution—is "no.") Nevertheless, if your transportation needs dictate that you finance a car, borrow as little as possible at the lowest rate you can find for the shortest period of time.

Beware of a dealer's promotional rates. An attractive interest rate can be used to distract you from an unattractive price. (Most car dealers, when interrogated, will eventually admit that you can get a better price if you pay cash than the dealer incentive rate.) Remember that banks and credit unions also offer attractive interest rates. Avoid buying a dealer's extended warranties or accident insurance; the dealer's price is not worth the benefits. Similarly, credit life insurance—which pays off the loan balance if you die—is only a good deal if you are terminally ill, but then there is a pre-existing condition clause that may apply to bar recovery.

Unless you have your own business and intend to use the

car for business travel, do not lease. While leasing a car requires the least cash down, you are paying the most to finance the car over the long run with no equity (or paid-up used car) to show for it in the end.

Home Equity Loan

This involves a line of credit secured by your home that you may draw upon and pay back, in full or in part, as often as you like. This financing method can be just as advantageous as it can be dangerous. If you are someone who has difficulty with controlling your credit-card spending, don't refinance your home. Think about it: it's like having a huge credit card with a longer time to repay. If there's nothing forcing you to pay off that new car you purchased with your equity line of credit, you probably won't, and you will be tempted to sink deeper into debt. And because the line of credit is tied to the general level of interest rates, when rates go up, so will your payment. If you can't pay, there goes your home in foreclosure. Home equity loans are designed for the self-disciplined borrower. The best terms are those with no points (service

> Ruben and his wife paid off their student loans, credit cards, and car loans with a home equity loan. The resulting new, larger home equity mortgage payment required two incomes. Unfortunately, they divorced. Neither could afford to keep the home and they had no equity, so when the home sold, they had nothing to show for it.

fees a lender will charge upfront to make the loan and to make a profit), and minimal upfront fees.

Credit Scores: Information That Goes into Them and How to Improve Them

As you probably know, lenders and others will look to your credit score to determine whether to extend you a loan, credit card, and set the interest rate. A credit score can also affect whether a landlord will rent you an apartment, and even the amount of a deposit you have to pay for utilities. The score is based on information that is reported to three credit bureaus (Equifax, Experian, and Trans Union) by past and current creditors about your financial history, as well as independent companies. The most commonly used method to determine your score is the FICO® score. FICO scores range from 300–850. The higher the score, the easier it will be for you to obtain credit at a low interest rate. Most lenders classify FICO credit scores above 700 as very good and an indication of good financial health. Below 620, on the other hand, usually places a borrower in the "subprime" category. This category translates to higher interest rates and applications could be turned down. Of the three credit bureaus that maintain credit information about you, each determines its own score for you. Lenders and others purchase credit reports about you from these bureaus to determine, among other things, whether to extend credit, rent to you, or adjust your credit card interest rate. If information changes at the bureau about your financial history, then your credit report changes—which means you always have the opportunity to improve your score.

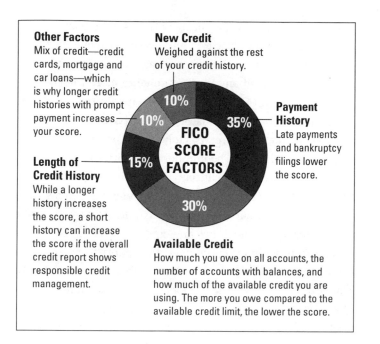

Other Factors
Mix of credit—credit cards, mortgage and car loans—which is why longer credit histories with prompt payment increases your score.

New Credit
Weighed against the rest of your credit history.

10%

10%

FICO SCORE FACTORS

35%

Payment History
Late payments and bankruptcy filings lower the score.

Length of Credit History
While a longer history increases the score, a short history can increase the score if the overall credit report shows responsible credit management.

15%

30%

Available Credit
How much you owe on all accounts, the number of accounts with balances, and how much of the available credit you are using. The more you owe compared to the available credit limit, the lower the score.

Because a FICO score covers various types of information, no one factor will determine your score. As the information in your credit report changes, so does the importance of the factors in determining your score.

Lenders also look at several other things when making a credit decision—income, length of time at your present job, and the type of credit for which you are applying. Nevertheless, improving your credit score can improve the picture lenders see of your creditworthiness and thus, qualify you for lower interest rates. There are six ways to improve your credit score: (1) Pay bills on time; (2) Since high debt levels hurt your score, pay off monthly balances, or at least, get the balances low on credit cards and avoid revolving balances; (3) Pay down the cards that are maxed-out first, because points are deducted any time you charge more than 50 percent of the limit; (4) Get current and stay current on debts, because the longer your history shows payment of bills on time, the better the score; (5) Only apply for new accounts if you really need them. The number of inquiries made for new account or loan applications results in a lower score, because when consumers anticipate money problems they try to increase their credit lines; (6) Review your credit report annually for accuracy and contact the credit reporting bureau from whom you obtained the report to correct any errors or omissions you find, along with the creditor. Verify that "closed by consumer" appears for all accounts you've closed. Checking on your own credit report does not negatively affect your score, only the inquiries and frequencies of others pulling your credit report are factored.

Sometimes the very things can advance a healthy financial future—such as not using credit cards and paying a debt off—can negatively affect your credit score. Lenders will tell you that not using credit cards, closing accounts, and transferring debt to the credit card with the lowest interest rate make it difficult for the credit-scoring formula to generate a score for you. However, you don't have to owe balances and pay interest to have a good score, you just have to use credit once in a while, as in, make a purchase when you know you'll be able to pay off the charged item during the grace period. The negative effect of closing an account will be minor if you have a high credit score. It will be major if you have a troubled financial history, but if you close out your accounts slowly over several months and close out your newest accounts first so that you don't lose the longer credit history, you can reduce the negative effect on your score. When weighing the potential negative effect of closing an account to becoming debt-free, consider that if your credit history is troubled or you've maxed out your credit limit, that's all the more reason to work on paying off the debt, rather than trying to acquire more credit and generate even more debt. After all, both positive and negative information go into your credit report, so your credit scores can change when new information is reported by your creditors. If you have late payments on your report, but re-establish a good record of making payments on time, your score will increase. This means, for a debt-ridden graduate, the score will inevitably improve over time so long as credit is managed responsibly.

You have the right to see what the bureaus are reporting about you when they provide a lender with a credit report. Under the Fair and Accurate Credit Transactions Act, Equifax, Experian, and Trans Union credit bureaus are required to provide consumers with a free credit report, once a year, upon the consumer's request. Though scores are built on changing information (for example, pay off a credit balance and your score increases, apply for a new account and your score decreases), most FICO scores change around twenty points a quarter. When you conduct your annual review of your financial status, go ahead and order your credit report. An annual review will help to correct errors and will also alert you to unauthorized transactions.

Avoid Piggybacking

Piggybacking is a controversial method for potentially boosting your credit score. You are listed as an authorized user on someone else's credit card whose credit history is healthy. You don't get to use the credit card, but the credit history of that card appears on your credit report making your report more attractive. Internet sites offering these techniques pay the credit holders who are making their credit available. The consumer with the damaged score pays the Internet site a hefty fee, and some may even be offered a high-interest credit line for use.

The practice is controversial because some argue it violates Federal Trade Commission and banking laws, and supports identity theft of those who are offering up their credit histories. Others counter that it's no different than getting someone to co-sign a loan. If you decide to do it, don't believe everything you read on the company's web site, especially with respect to money-back guarantees, and pull your credit report to ensure that information is being correctly reported. Before you sign up, however, consider that the money you'd use to pay the site would likely be put to a better purpose: paying down your debt.

It should be mentioned that even if you trust the person adding you to his or her card, some credit companies will refuse to report you—even as an authorized user— to the credit bureaus. The cardholder should ask whether the credit history will be reported to the appropriate bureaus for you; if not, there's no point in risking the credit history of someone you trust—should you make purchases and default, which will then bring down your Good Samaritan's credit score. Bottom line: Borrowing another's record can be risky for everyone involved.

Sources and Resources

www.financenter.com (Offers a calculator to help choose the best credit card.)

www.fincalc.com (Financial calculators.)

http://www.wsmv.com/video/10417539/detail.html (11/28/06, video from WSMV in Nashville showing how to use a script to reduce interest rate. Script to Negotiate a Lower Credit Card Rate: Hi, my name is _____. I am a good customer but I have received several offers in the mail from other credit card companies with lower annual percentage rates. I want a lower rate on my credit card. What can you do to help me?

If they say they can't help, or if they offer a rate that's not low enough for you, ask: Is that the best you can do? If that's the best they can do, and it's still not low enough for you, then ask: May I speak to a supervisor please? Then repeat the same script with the supervisor.)

Tips on how to prevent identity theft and what can be done if you're a victim, can be found at *www.consumer.gov*, *www.ftc.gov*, and *www.privacyrights.org*.

The Secret History of the Credit Card Industry: *http://www.pbs.org/wgbh/pages/frontline/shows/credit*

Individual Credit Reporting Bureaus:

Equifax Web: *www.equifax.com*, Phone: 1 -800-685-1111

Experian Web: *www.experian.com*, Phone: 1 866-200-6020

TransUnion Web: *www.transunion.com*, Phone: 1-800-888-4213

freecreditreport.com (Provides you with a "free" credit report and credit score, yet enrolls you in a "trial membership" for its credit monitoring service. If you don't cancel the trial within thirty days, a $12.95 monthly fee will be incurred.)

AnnualCreditReport.com (Sponsored by the three major credit bureaus—Equifax, Experian, and TransUnion—provides you with one free credit report (but not your credit score) from each credit bureau over a period of twelve months.)

For More Information on Credit Repair Scams:

www.bbb.org (Better Business Bureau), *www.naag.org* (click on your state's Attorney General), *www.consumer world.org*

"Declaring Bankruptcy Can Improve Your Credit Score," by Aleksandra Todorova, *Smart Money* magazine, January 22, 2007: *http://www.smartmoney.com/debt/advice/index.cfm?story=boostscore*

Bankruptcy scenario, consider *In re Aprea* (Bkrtcy. E.D. Tex. May 18, 2007) (Chapter 13 debtor did not propose plan in good faith requiring dismissal. He used unsecured credit to finance his living expenses prior to bankruptcy, anticipated spending more than $700 per month on food and recreation, leased a new luxury vehicle for his fiancée, then proposed to pay one unsecured creditor for his fifty-inch TV, and surround-sound system, but pay only .005 percent of his remaining unsecured debt.)

For Car Purchases:

www.carbuyingtips.com (Car buying tips.)

www.carinfo.com (Car tips.)

www.consumerreports.org (Offers various tips on purchasing cars and other consumer items.)

www.kbb.com (Kelley Blue Book valuations.)

www.edmunds.com (Guide to what types of cars and models retain their value.)

Housing:
It's Not How Much Mortgage You Qualify For, but How Much You Can Comfortably Afford to Pay

*"To be an American is to aspire
to a room of one's own."*

New York Times,
"Dream House," April 19, 1987.

Let your budget be your guide in considering when to buy a home and how much home to buy. Ideally, you should have saved enough money for a 20 percent down payment (that's in addition to the emergency fund and maxing-out your annual retirement contribution), though lenders and realtors may tell you that a 5 percent to 10 percent down payment is sufficient if you have good credit and a job. However, just as home quality is not measured by square footage, neither is the quality of your life. There's no shame in renting a 500 square-foot studio if you're happy there. Quite simply, if you're not emotionally or financially ready to buy a home yet, don't do it just because society dictates that's what people do when they're your age.

Reasons to Rent

The common argument for owning over renting is that rent is money down the drain, while a mortgage builds equity and offers a tax deduction. Owning a home can also be a good inflation hedge. However, there are four arguments in support of renting: (1) your city's housing prices tend to be obscenely inflated (for example, New York City, Los Angeles, San Francisco); (2) you'll be moving in less than five years (sometimes it takes at least five years to recoup the money you pay in real estate broker commissions, loan fees and closing costs); (3) you don't have the time, money, or energy to personally handle the upkeep of a home; (4) a devastatingly low FICO score results in an onerously high interest rate (which adds hundreds of dollars per month to your mortgage payment), and you have no money to pay a large down payment or significant cash reserves saved.

The question of tax benefits is whether the mortgage-interest deduction cuts your taxes enough to make owning a place cheaper than renting one. Figure out the tax savings and determine whether it costs more to own than rent. If so, then the question to answer is whether the extra expense of owning a home (1) brings you greater enjoyment; and (2) the potential for the value of the property to appreciate.

Chapter Five

Buying a Home

When it comes to financial transactions, what matters most isn't the price, but what you're left paying, or receiving, after tax. As discussed more in Chapters Seven and Nine, taxes cut the true return on most investments. Moreover, tax savings can cut the true cost of the deductible expenses, if you have enough deductions to itemize. So, while real estate agents and loan officers may ply with you computations of how much mortgage you can qualify for to purchase the McMansion on the hill, consider these three issues: (1) the amount of the purchase price to borrow; (2) the monthly payment of a fifteen-year versus a thirty-year loan; and (3) the difference between a fixed and an adjustable rate mortgage (ARM). Examining these issues will help you determine what amount you can afford to comfortably pay for your home—meaning, after you buy your home, you don't want to be so financially strapped that you're unable to sleep at night or enjoy an occasional evening out.

Debt-to-Income Ratio for Conventional Mortgage[2]

As a general rule, a monthly mortgage payment (including principal, interest, real estate taxes, and homeowners insurance) should not exceed 28 percent of your gross monthly income.

---

2. FHA and VA government-backed loans have different debt-to-income ratios.

Gross Income	Housing Expense Max 28% Monthly	Debt-to-Income Max 36% Monthly
$50,000	$1,167	$1,500
$60,000	$1,400	$1,800
$70,000	$1,633	$2,100
$80,000	$1,867	$2,400
$90,000	$2,100	$2,700
$100,000	$2,333	$3,000
$125,000	$2,916	$3,750
$160,000	$3,733	$4,800

So, before you go home-shopping, calculate how much of a housing expense you can manage by multiplying your annual salary by .28, then divide by 12 (months). Next, calculate your total monthly debt obligation by multiplying your annual salary by .36, then divide by 12 (months). The result is your maximum allowable debt-to-income ratio. The debt obligation includes student loans, credit cards, car loan, child support and alimony, and the mortgage.

Three Approaches to Home Buying

Lenders offer different types of mortgage products. While no single loan is best for all situations, there are three approaches to keep in mind when selecting what kind of mortgage is right for your overall financial strategy.

Borrow as Little as Possible for as Short a Time as Possible

When you're shopping for a mortgage loan, consider this question: Why buy more of something than you need, espe-

Loan Term	Interest Rate	Loan Amount	Monthly Payment	Total Payments	Total Interest Paid
15 years	5.77%	$200,000	$1,662.96	$299,333.31	$99,333.31
30 years	6.0%	$200,000	$1,199.10	$431,676.38	$231,676.38

Assuming the above interest rates as an example, after 15 years, you've paid off, and in effect, saved up $200,000 with the 15-year loan. Yet, with a 30-year loan, after 15 years of payments, you'll only have paid off/saved up $52,685.38. Scrape together an extra $250 per month to pay to principal for the 30-year, it'll be paid in 20 years, saving $91,317.81 in interest.

cially if the product costs more than what you could earn if you saved the money? Think of a fifteen-year loan as a forced savings program: after fifteen years, you'll have paid off the loan, and have essentially saved the value of your home, increasing your net worth. If you are unable to qualify for a fifteen-year, take out the thirty-year and pay extra to principal each month to accomplish the same goal. Make certain that there are no pre-payment penalties associated with the thirty-year, however.

Also, consider that for most twenty- and thirty-something, the average homeowner stays in his or her first home for seven years before selling and moving again. Therefore, the fifteen-year loan would allow you to save more equity, which can be favorably applied to the purchase of the next home. Regarding whether to choose a fixed or adjustable rate mortgage, if the rates and fees for both types of mortgages are the same, go with the fixed, because the risk of an adjustable rate soaring and creating an out-of-control monthly payment is eliminated.

Adjustable rate mortgages (ARMs) are tied to one of two independent indices: U.S. Treasury securities or the cost that banks and savings and loans pay to borrow funds. A margin of 2 to 3 percent is added to the index rate, resulting in the mortgage rate for an "adjustment period." The adjustment period is the amount of time between rate adjustments. Only when interest rates are high and the adjustable rate is considerably cheaper, with a cap on how much the rate can rise in any one year and over the life of the loan, should an ARM be selected over the fixed rate. (In essence, refinancing achieves the same goal as taking out an adjustable rate mortgage when rates are at an all-time high: that is, as the rates drop, you benefit by a better rate). There's also the "convertible" adjustable rate, which provides an option of locking in a fixed rate after a specified number of years, when interest rates have fallen. But the adjustable rate mortgage is the cheapest, according to the broker or loan officer, right? Well, the adjustable rate market can be deceptive. A low initial rate is usually a promotion. The important question is, what will the rate be after the first adjustment? Practically speaking, after the first adjustment occurs is when the loan is starting— not at the come-hither rate—and that's the number you should use when comparing alternatives. Also, make certain that the cap on the adjustable rate is not just on your monthly payments. There can be a back-ended situation where any excess above the cap may be tacked on as additional principal; consequently, additional monthly payments are added to the back end of the loan (a thirty-year loan becomes a thirty-two-year) or the monthly payment stays high long after interest rates have dropped. As to fixed and adjustable rates, lenders are continually creating new products every week, but remember this pearl of wisdom that is common to all: If you cannot afford a higher fixed-rate loan, you cannot afford to be buying the home. If it is true that, but for the low initial rate promoted by the adjustable rate mortgage, you can't pay your monthly payments, walk away.

Max-out the Amount Borrowed and the Term

Often, new homeowners will take out the maximum amount the lender says they qualify for at the longest term (thirty-year) so they can afford more house. Don't fall into this trap. This method only makes sense for the truly wealthy as a financial strategy, not as a strategy for those financially struggling to buy more house. If you lock-in a bargain thirty-year fixed rate, when rates zoom up, you're protected. When rates plunge, the loan can be paid off and refinanced at a lower rate. The wealthy can afford to do this because paying additional closing costs for the refinancing is chump-change for them, and they're not forced to sell the home to pay for the next one if their work or lifestyle requires them to move.

For those who have to make their paychecks stretch to accomplish their financial goals (and just pay the bills month-to-month), this method is less advantageous because it builds little equity if you have to sell in less than ten years. Furthermore, it is more expensive in the long run with your paying interest to the lender instead of your savings or advancing your investments. In fact, many fall into the trap of first scraping together the down payment and closing costs, and then going even more into debt by using credit cards to deck out their new home and fund living expenses. If you choose this method, make sure you have enough of a financial cushion to max-out the annual retirement contributions and save for other financial goals. Though the urge to splurge on decor and new furnishings for your new home may be great, if you can't pay cash for it, don't buy it. Otherwise, the dream home will likely propel you into financial struggles for a very long time.

Borrow Nothing at All

If you can afford to, when the cost of borrowing is high, it may be better to borrow nothing at all. After all, in negotiations, a cash offer can carve a few thousand off the purchase price. Average costs for a mortgage are $3,000 per $200,000 loan, along with the time expended completing the application process. This method makes sense when your after-tax calculations show that the money you have sitting in investments is earning less than a mortgage would cost you. Built into this method is the carefree feeling of being debt-free, which is a plus for those with nervous stomachs. Of course, you'd still leave enough in your account for the emergency fund discussed in Chapter One. It should also be mentioned that if you choose this method, don't waive the home inspection. Regardless of how much you love the home, a professional building inspector can identify unseen problems that are inherent in the property. (Watch the movie the *Money Pit* if you doubt the importance of this endeavor.)

Other Considerations before Applying for a Mortgage

Before you begin the mortgage application process, be aware of these practices:

Online Lending

The Internet is a good resource for researching rates and fees. Those who don't have a high FICO score are likely to find brokers as the source of best rates for them. However, be careful, because brokers will be charging a fee for matching you with a lender.

Annual Percentage Rate (APR)

APR is the annual finance charge, which includes the costs for loan origination fees, mortgage insurance, and points. The points are a percentage of the loan that you pay upfront to "buy down" the interest rate on the mortgage. One point equals 1 percent of the loan and typically lowers the interest rate by 1/4 percent (for example, one point on a $200,000 loan would be $2,000). Paying points makes sense if you won't be selling the home in less than five to ten years; otherwise, it's unlikely you'll have the time to recoup the costs. When comparing interest rates for fixed rates, you have to take into consideration the APR and points to understand what the true cost of the loan will be. A seemingly low interest rate doesn't necessary mean it's the best deal for you without comparing the APR for rates and fees. Because the rate used for the ARM will likely change with interest rates, the APR cannot be used for a long-term comparison, however.

Credit Report

A FICO score in the 500 range is generally the minimum that will qualify for a mortgage. If you're about to apply for a loan, keep the credit card accounts open so that there's less likelihood that a closed account would decrease your score. (Keeping it open for purposes of a loan application does not mean charging it up, sabotaging your debt-free goals.) For the reasons discussed in Chapter Four, it is imperative that your credit history be the best possible before you apply for a mortgage. This includes making certain that the report's information is accurate. A 2004 study found one out of four people had serious errors on their credit reports, so make certain you are not that unfortunate person before applying for a loan. Also, don't pad the region with loan applications, because that will lead to multiple inquiries for your credit report. The frequency of inquiries can decrease the FICO score that a lender will consider in making the loan. Your own inquiries about your credit report will not count against you, so review your credit reports for any mistakes before applying for a loan.

House-poor

Typically, the maximum loan you'll qualify for is always greater than what you can comfortably afford to pay on a monthly basis. If the lender tells you that you qualify for a mortgage whose payment is greater than your rent, yet you're barely getting by paying rent, you obviously shouldn't take out a mortgage that will be greater than your rental payment. Likewise, it's easy to be persuaded by a realtor that you'll grow into a house, but that doesn't mean that your paycheck will grow, too. Years of sacrificing dinners out, travel, and other pleasures to pay the mortgage can transform your dream house into a prison. Buying a home that is less expensive frees you to enjoy fun things without getting over your head in credit-card debt. Paying extra to principal for an early pay-off of your mortgage is also an option. Keep this general rule as a backdrop when talking with lenders and realtors: the sales price should be less than two-and-a-half times your income. For illustration purposes, this means that if your income is $60,000, then the home price should be $150,000 or under.

Job History

Be prepared if the lender asks you for a letter showing that you've satisfied the probationary period of your job if you've been there less than a year. Applicants with years at the same job are more likely to be approved than those who have been hopping from job to job. The exception is if you're switching jobs within the same occupation for higher salaries.

Refinancing an Existing Mortgage

But for the cost of paying points and closing costs, home-owners would refinance an existing fixed-rate mortgage every time the rates drop. The question becomes whether it's worth the closing costs and effort to refinance. If refinancing will knock off 2 percent from your fixed interest rate, and the points and mortgage interest are fully deductible, maybe it's worth it to you. As with everything, do your research and analyze what is the best deal. For example, compare a 6.5 percent loan that charges no points to a 6.25 percent loan that charges 1.5 points. The first loan costs less initially, but after awhile, the savings at the basic rate of 6.5 percent may outweigh the points you paid upfront if you hold the loan for a long period. So, if you expect to be holding the loan for a long time, take the 6.25 percent loan that charges 1.5 points; otherwise, the 6.5 percent would be the better option, especially if you intended to move in five to ten years. Just as with other mortgages, shop around, but ask your lender what's available first to see if it is willing to offer the best rate to keep your business.

Sources and Resources

"Mortgage Brokers: Friend or Foe," By James Hagarty, *Wall Street Journal* Online, May 30, 2007 (*www.wsj.com*)

"The Real Estate Generation Gap," *Boston Globe*, March 25, 2007, *www.boston.com*

www.hud.gov (Offers information on buying a home and buying programs in your state.)

Mortgage Calculators: *http://money.cnn.com*; *www.bankrate.com*; *www.quicken.com*; *www.mortgage101.com*; *www.realtor.com*; *www.priceline.com*

For a printable/downloadable worksheet of questions to ask mortgage lenders, go to *www.bankrate.com* and search for "Work sheet: interviewing mortgage lenders."

"Consumer Handbook on Adjustable Rate Mortgages," Federal Reserve Board, *www.federalreserve.gov/pubs/brochure.htm*

"How to Shop for a Mortgage," Mortgage Bankers Association of America, *www.mbaa.org*

Home Inspections: National Association of Home Inspectors, *www.nahi.org*

Bankruptcy and the Danger of Buying More Home than You Need or Can Afford: *In re Loper*, (Bkrtcy D. Colo. May 18, 2007) (Chapter 13 debtors failed to establish that retention of their home, with its associated expense, was reasonably necessary. Thus, confirmation of their plan was not warranted, despite the debtors' contention that their home was one of the least expensive in the area. The debtors were spending $5,690 per month on a home in which they had little or no equity. The housing costs devoured two-thirds of their monthly net income. The plan provided for payment of less than 10 percent of their unsecured debt.)

When Your Iceberg Melts:
Insuring for Catastrophes

"If something can go wrong, it will."
Murphy's Law

Just as Murphy's Law can occur at anytime in trial practice, so it can in life. If you're thinking, "I can skip this chapter because I'm healthy," don't. That's not to suggest that you'll end up like the lawyer in *Regarding Henry* (Hollywood's stereotypical depiction of a New York lawyer who must suffer a brain injury before he can be transformed from a malevolent narcissist into a decent person), but accidents, crimes, and injuries can happen to lawyers, not just the parties they represent. Luckily, certain types of insurance coverage can buffer the financial strain when they do.

Health Insurance

Regardless of your age, you need health insurance. If you are simply unable to afford the premiums, search for a policy with a very high deductible to limit your financial exposure. An example of a high deductible is $5,000. However, even with the rising costs of health insurance, group plans through an employer are generally the cheapest option. When you're fortunate to be young and healthy, a local insurance agent may be able to find you something cheaper with insurance companies that factor age when setting rates. However, be sure to ask what proportion of the premiums collected is actually allocated to pay claims. If the number isn't available in writing, it's usually because up to 50 percent of the premiums collected don't go to pay claims.

When you reach fifty-five, group coverage is available through the American Association of Retired Persons (AARP). If insurers deem you uninsurable because of your health history, you may be able to buy health insurance through a state's risk pool.

HMO vs. PPO

Most employer group health plans will be HMO or PPO plans. A health maintenance organization (HMO) and a preferred provider organization (PPO) are both managed-care plans. HMOs are the most prevalent form of managed care. In managed care, all health services and financing go through one organization. Services include inpatient, outpatient care, and prescription drug benefits. The HMO requires insured members to use its network of hospitals and health-care professionals. These health-care professionals are either employed by or under contract to the HMO. Members pay a monthly fee that changes only if the entire fee structure changes annually, regardless of the care they may need.

PPOs are less restrictive than HMOs. A PPO consists of a group of hospitals and health-care professionals who agree to provide care to members at a reduced cost. The benefit of a PPO is flexibility for its members, who do not have to use the services within the network, but the costs encourage them to do so. Staying within the network means that your costs are lower. When members seek medical care outside the network, they are still covered but must pay a higher deductible and contribute a higher co-payment. Be sure you know what each system offers so you can estimate your actual healthcare costs.

If your healthcare options include the choice between an HMO and a PPO, you will need to determine whether your physicians participate and, if not, whether you will be able to afford your share of their fee if you opt for a PPO. The value of continuity in using a physician you've seen for years may provide for more secure diagnoses and would favor paying outside of the network medical care. HMOs and PPOs may monitor and sometimes limit the services and care that its physicians provide to members. Thus, the headline-generating controversy: Managed-care plans may determine that the medical treatment a member's physician recommends is unnecessary and expensive, resulting in denial of a claim. Do not make the mistake of thinking that because your doctor recommends a procedure, the insurer automatically will pay for it. It's not uncommon for an insurer to, in effect, second-guess a doctor and deem a treatment too expensive, ineffective, or unnecessary. That's not to say you can't do your research, fight the insurer's decision, and possibly win. How-

> Erin prefers a PPO because of a medical condition that requires specialized care, and because PPO members do not need a referral before seeing a specialist. However, for Nate, ongoing out-of-pocket costs are his primary concern, so HMO is a better choice because there are no deductibles and co-payments are typically lower.

ever, it is another reason supporting the establishment of an emergency fund, discussed in Chapters One and Two, before indulging, pampering or splurging on "wanted" but not "needed" items.

Nevertheless, if you have a choice between HMO and PPO, take time to evaluate the coverage offered by each, and determine which best suits the needs of you and your family.

COBRA

If you lose your job, make sure to notify your employer (or your spouse's employer) within sixty days of your intention to elect COBRA benefits so that you can continue your health insurance benefits. Familiarize yourself with what is considered a "qualifying event" under the Consolidated Omnibus Reconciliation Act (COBRA) of 1986, and when coverage can end. (If you lose your job for cause or misconduct, COBRA is inapplicable.) The Health Insurance Portability and Accountability Act of 1986 (HIPAA) may also come into play if there is a pre-existing condition issue with your health history. Also, read your employer's Summary Plan Description and plan booklets that spell out the coverage, your rights, and your responsibilities.

Disability Insurance

Group disability insurance coverage is usually available through your employer for a minimal cost. Paid with pre-tax dollars, it may offer short- or long-term disability coverage to keep your income stream going when you are unable to work due to illness of injury. Disability coverage is measured in time. An insurer will scrutinize an injury or illness, asking, will the policyholder be back to work in six months, a year, or never? Coverage may kick in (a) the moment your illness or injury renders you temporarily or permanently disabled, or (b) months after you've been diagnosed with a temporary or permanent disability. Route (a) will be the most expensive premium, but offers the best coverage. Defining "disabled" as the inability to do your regular work versus doing *any* work is the policy you want to find, though you may not have much choice if you're buying disability insurance through a group plan offered by your employer.

Whether to purchase a different policy or an additional back-up policy independent of your employer depends on the (1) the language of your employer's group disability policy in defining "disabled"[3] and how it pays benefits (that is, the per-

3. Group disability policies tend to have a liberal definition of "disabled" for the first two years; then, insurers tend to become more restrictive with definitions limiting your disabled status to whether you are unable to perform *a* job, as opposed to *your* job. If you can be gainfully employed in some sense, the insurer may likely challenge your disabled status. So, ask for a copy of the policy from your employer and understand the applicable restrictions so you know whether to obtain additional coverage, along with researching other companies (independent of your employer's group insurer) that will provide coverage when your income drops because of disability.

Jack earned a $130,000 salary. At the insistence of his well-intentioned, albeit nagging mother, he signed up for the group disability policy. It limited his benefits to $5,000 per month ($60,000 per year). His budget fixed expenses at $75,000 a year. To cover the $15,000 gap, he wrapped an individual policy around the group coverage so there would be no shortage in his income stream if he became disabled. His mother had keen foresight: after a fall on the ski slope, he experienced excruciating back pain so severe it required two separate surgeries, disabling him for nearly twenty-four months.

centage of your paycheck, short-term or long-term, the elimination period); (2) health history and lifestyle; and (3) family obligations. Long-term disability policies pay benefits for several years or until the age of sixty-five. Short-term policies pay benefits for a shorter period of time, usually six weeks to two years. The shorter the elimination period and the longer the benefit period, the higher the premium. A standard policy will replace 60 percent of your income, up to a maximum of $5,000 to $10,000 per month.

An important tax consideration is that if you pay your own disability premiums, and subsequently become disabled, the disability payments are not taxable. However, if the premiums are paid by your employer, then you will be taxed on the benefits. If the employer policy does not cover your expenses, then it's usually a good idea to purchase on your own a policy that will allow you to be made financially whole, instead of experiencing a shortfall in earnings, if you were unable to work because a medical condition, illness, or injury rendered you disabled. Ask about a "wrap-around" policy for the group disability coverage with your employer, or find another carrier to provide a policy that would provide the full benefits you need.

If you think you don't need the extra expense of a disability policy, consider that, according to the Social Security Administration, a twenty-something worker has a 30 percent chance of becoming disabled before retirement. For a thirty-year-old, the risk is 4.1 times more likely than death. Bottom line: The greatest asset you have is your ability to produce income. Insure it just as you would any other valuable item.

Life Insurance

If you have a child or significant other who is financially dependent upon your income, buy life insurance. Otherwise, save your money. When deciding how much life insurance to buy, the general rule is that you'll need between five to ten times your annual salary. For a more exact calculation, ask yourself these questions: (1) How much of my annual income will my heirs need to replace me? For most, the answer is 75 percent of your annual take-home pay, rather than 100 percent, because they will no longer have to pay for your food, clothes, and Starbucks® or gadget habit. (2) What is the annual social security benefit, if any, my heirs could expect to receive? The gap, if any, between the answers to questions 1 and 2, will be what you want the life insurance to cover. (3) How long will my heirs need to fill the gap? Consider the ages

Multiply the annual income gap by the figure on the right that corresponds to how long your heirs will need to fill the gap.	
5 years	4.7
10 years	9
15 years	12
20 years	15
25 years	18
30 years	20
50 years	26

of your heirs when deciding how long the proceeds will have to cover a gap in income. For example, if you have children in school, estimate how much longer they will need financial support. Assuming that your heirs can invest the proceeds at a 3 percent rate of return after taxes and inflation, calculate the amount of coverage needed from the table, above.

For example, assuming that your annual take-home pay is $100,000, your heirs can make do with $75,000, and social security will put in $15,000 until your children turn 18. To provide an additional $60,000 for ten years would mean $540,000 of coverage. Factor in an additional six months' salary for funeral expenses, grief-induced leave of employment for your heirs, and any other concerns for which payment would be needed. Subtract from this amount the salary of your surviving significant other, assets you've accumulated, such as interest, stock dividends, your retirement account. As a general rule of thumb, you should also add in a cushion of $25,000 to $50,000, if you have children. The resulting number is the amount of life insurance coverage to buy.

Next, look for the cheapest, annual renewable term life insurance. Term insurance is not an investment—it offers no cash value—but it has two advantages for twenty-, thirty- and forty-somethings. First, it's cheap, and second, you're not locked in. If you ever decide to drop the policy or switch to another, there's no penalty. The disadvantage is that it will become expensive as you get older (because with age, the probability increases that you may actually die and the beneficiaries will expect payment). Term insurance is what most employers offer. It is generally in force only during the period of your employment. Typically, an employer's insurance will cover one to two times your annual salary, though you may be allowed to purchase additional coverage at a group rate that is lower than you would find on your own.

Insurance companies also market whole-life-type products that combine insurance and investments. The argument favoring a whole-life policy is that it forces you to save. You pay an extra premium upfront when you're young, then, as you age, the amount of coverage your money buys will shrink, with the savings you've built up, via the policy, expanding to take its place. A disadvantage is that if what you're really looking for is an investment, you're usually better off buying the term insurance, then using excess money you'd have been paying with the whole life, and depositing in an IRA, or pay off your home mortgage. The sales fees—loaded into the whole life product—can be high in comparison with the rate of return. Another problem with whole life is that most people let the policies lapse, losing the money they've paid in, or incur a large penalty for early withdrawal.[4]

---

4. If a salesperson argues that term life is a waste of money because only a small percentage of people ever collect, consider that, under that logic, it would seem that few people ever collect on car or fire insurance for their home, but it would be irresponsible not to protect your property.

For all policies, ask the following questions: (1) What expenses are covered? (2) What are the deductibles, co-payments, and stop-loss provisions? (3) What conditions or treatments are covered by the deductible? (4) What is the company's maximum for payments? (5) Are there conditions and services (interior limits within the policy) that aren't covered? (6) Is the plan guaranteed renewable and noncancelable?

The crucial issue with whole-life products is what rate of interest you will be paid on the savings portion, assuming a good, low rate on the insurance portion of the policy. To the extent an insurer provides glossy illustrations showing premiums vanishing as money is compounding, consider whether the money is backed by volatile investments in which you ordinarily wouldn't put your hard-earned paycheck. Generally, the premium goes toward the insurance coverage, administrative fees, and the cash value of your investment, but you have no control over how the insurance company invests the cash value, unless it is variable universal life insurance. With variable universal life insurance, consumers can build cash value just as with the whole-life product, but are able to manage their own money by investing in a variety of accounts, similar to mutual funds. Variable products can bring certain tax advantages, though they do come with fees. So, careful analysis of whether the tax consequences are beneficial in comparison with the fees charged and rate of return is necessary before committing funds. The bottom line: If you want insurance coverage, buy term insurance. If you want to invest your money, read Chapter Seven. Nevertheless, if you're convinced a whole-life or variable universal life policy is the way to go, find a fee-only, independent insurance agent, who, for a fixed fee, will research the various policies and make a recommendation about the one that's best for you. The agent should not be receiving a commission, to ensure objectivity. As with any investment, calculate what the rate of return will be, after taxes, to determine whether a combined insurance and savings product will help you achieve your financial goals.

Long-Term Care

Health and disability policies may not cover long-term care such as home health care, nursing home, or assisted-living facilities, and adult daycare. While long-term care may appear to be for the elderly, the young may find the need if a debilitating illness or accident occurs with no nearby family or financial savings to handle the care responsibilities.[5] In short, the longer you live, the more likely you'll need long-term care. According to a *New England Journal of Medicine* report, 10 percent of men and 18 percent of women may need nursing home care for one-to-five years. For obvious reasons, the younger you are, the more likely you are to qualify for benefits. Opting for fewer benefits or a shorter benefit waiting period may trim premium costs, as well as extending the

---

5. It should be noted that Medicare is not a long-term option because it does not cover custodial-care expenses.

elimination (waiting) period or increasing the deductible. It is worth mentioning that if a couple buys two policies, some companies will waive the premium for the second policy once benefits for the first policy activate. However, at this stage of your career, if handling the basic living expenses is proving difficult, adding long-term care insurance payments is likely not advisable.

Products to Avoid

Don't buy credit life or cancer insurance. It's nearly always cheaper to purchase one comprehensive, all-purpose policy. Also, be cautious of rate structures that (1) offer incredibly low first-year rates, yet have high rates thereafter; and (2) look great, but may be raised at the discretion of the insurer. If you're healthy and enjoy taking a risk, "reversionary term" offers good rates for those in good health; however, the insured will be required to requalify every five years or less. If your health deteriorates, they may insure you, but at higher rates. You, of course, are free to seek a better rate elsewhere if your health deteriorates, but the danger is that the new insurer's pre-existing condition clause may bar coverage for the very illness or condition you want insured.

Property Insurance

If you own a car or home, you have to insure them. The trick is not overpaying for coverage and ensuring that you have sufficient coverage before an accident, fire, or flood occurs.

Insuring Your Car

How much insurance you must buy often depends on the state you live in. The majority of states require that drivers purchase, at least, the state's minimum bodily-injury liability, which will pay your medical bills and lost wages, along with the medical bills of others hurt in an accident that you are shown to have caused, and property damage up to whatever limits you choose. For example, some states require at least 20/40/10. (The first number equals the bodily-injury liability maximum for one person injured in an accident, the second number bodily-injury liability maximum for all injuries in one accident, and the third number is for property-damage liability maximum for one accident). A 20/40/10 requirement translates to $20,000 of coverage per person, $40,000 of coverage for more than one person, and $10,000 for property damage. Personal injury or medical coverage pays your own medical costs if you're injured in an accident. It is recommended that, unless you have no assets, you should at least have limits of 100/300 for bodily injury to sufficiently cover your medical costs and possible lost wages.

The Internet is a great resource for comparing rates and locating the best deal in your region. Check the deductibles and don't pay for unnecessary extras. For example, collision coverage pays for repairing your car if you hit something, so don't buy it if you have a beat-up clunker. Likewise, when you have good health insurance, medical coverage may not be necessary. Nevertheless, if you have assets to protect, buy enough liability insurance to do so. When you have a good driving record, you may be able to significantly lower your premium by a high deductible of $500 to $1,000.

Insuring Your Home

Shop around for the best rates and consider the deductibles. Do insure your home for at least 80 percent of its replacement cost (even partial losses will not be considered fully covered). Review your policy every year to be certain that you aren't paying for more (or less) coverage than needed. To the extent you would have to rebuild your home if it were completely destroyed, be sure that you increase the limits as the cost associated with homebuilding increases. This can be done through an inflation rider that will increase the coverage annually at the rate of inflation. Also, add $1 million in liability insurance for slip-and-falls (because chances are, when your new neighbor learns that you are one of those high-priced lawyers, he will ask for pain and suffering incurred from falling on your porch while dropping off your welcome neighbor basket).

"Replacement cost coverage" will increase the premium, but it is usually worth it. This is because if your high-definition TV is stolen, you'll want to replace it with a new one, as opposed to "actual cash value," which will only pay the cost of the TV when you first purchased it. List all valuables such as jewelry, antiques, silverware, and the like, that you want covered in a schedule attached to the policy. If you have a business-related office set-up at home, your homeowners (or renters) policy likely won't cover a stolen computer or scanner without a special endorsement for it. So, ask your agent

> Conduct an annual review of your homeowners insurance, confirming that: (1) the specific features of the policy are right for you; (2) you're including everything that you need to for coverage; (3) the amount of insurance is sufficient given any changes in your status in life and the value of your property; and (4) the policy is priced competitively for what if offers.

for a separate quote. Also, some insurers offer discounts for precautionary measures such as smoke detectors, fire extinguishers, deadbolts, or alarm systems. Homeowners insurance does not cover land, so, when deciding how much to purchase, exclude the land value from your calculation. Finally, flood insurance should be considered when your home is located near water or could be considered "near water" once in a great while. Typically, flood insurance requires that a full year's premium be paid up to five days in advance before coverage will be in effect. Unless the home is sold, cancellation will not be permitted mid-year (as in when the home survives the rainy season unscathed).

Umbrella Policy

An umbrella policy is essentially extended personal-liability coverage. If your liability policy stops at $500,000 but the accident victim sues you for $1 million, the umbrella policy comes into play. It covers almost any noncriminal activity you could be sued for that's unrelated to your business or

> When a guest drowned in Jeff's backyard swimming pool, an umbrella policy alleviated the financial consequences.

profession. For example, Clark Griswold needed an umbrella policy when an elderly uncle's simple act of lighting a cigar near Clark's brittle tree set the uncle on fire in the movie, *Christmas Vacation*. Even though it seems unlikely that you'll ever need the shelter of an umbrella policy, if you have assets to protect, you should buy this as supplemental coverage; at least $1 million worth of personal liability coverage. Under certain circumstances, some umbrella policies will kick in where an insured's auto liability policy stopped. As with all contracts, read the fine print to understand the restrictions before buying.

Renters Insurance

If you have valuables that you can't afford to replace if they were lost or stolen, you should buy renters insurance.

Insuring Children

Don't bother. Life insurance is to replace the income earned by the policyholder so that any financial strain is eliminated or, at least, lessened for the policyholder's dependents. Unless you have income-producing children or your children have dependents, they don't need life insurance. The money can be put toward one of your other financial goals.

Deductibles

When comparing insurance premiums for the best deal, ask what you'd save by opting for the highest deductible. With respect to property, the big risks are the ones you want to be protected against—destruction of your home by fire, for example—not the little ones. So, a higher deductible may be worth the risk and cost-analysis. With respect to your health, whether a high deductible is best depends on your individual circumstances. If you're young and healthy, you may be able to afford a higher deductible. But, if you have a family member who is prone to illness, the higher deductible will cause you to incur significant out-of-pocket expenses.

Health Savings Accounts (HSAs)

The Medicare Prescription Drug, Improvement and Modernization Act of 2003 set up HSAs for qualified medical expenses. An HSA is like an IRA for medical expenses; an eligible individual who is covered under a high-deductible health plan can contribute the amount of the annual deductible on a tax-deductible basis. Distributions can be made at any time so long as they are for qualified medical expenses. HSAs make high-deductible medical plans a cheaper alternative, and are worth researching for eligibility and compatibility with your circumstances.

Inventory

Take an inventory of your household belongings, along with photos or video of everything, so you'll have a readily avail-

> Andrea accidentally hit a deer while driving. It caused substantial damage to her car and she filed a claim. The following month, when hail cracked her windshield, she opted to pay for the damage out-of-pocket rather than risk a rise in her rates by the insurer.

able way to prove your losses should there be a fire or other damage. A fire-proof safe or safe-deposit box in a safe location is appropriate for storing the insurance inventory and accompanying photos or video.

To File or Not to File

Insurers will likely raise your rates and charge higher premiums if you file claims, regardless of whether the damage caused was your fault. It may seem unfair, but that's the way it is. Remember, you're really buying insurance coverage to protect from catastrophic losses that pose a financial disaster. So, before you file a claim, consider whether it's small enough for you to cover out-of-pocket, rather than risking a higher premium at year's end or, in some circumstances, a refusal by the insurer to renew your policy altogether.

The FICO Score Practice

While a few states prohibit auto and home insurers from using credit scoring formulas to help determine premiums, the controversial practice continues elsewhere. The reason is that researchers have found a correlation between how well people handle credit and how likely they are to cost the insurer money. The presumption is that a high credit score translates to fewer claims filed. Thus, if your credit history is shaky, an insurer may deem you more likely to file claims and you will pay higher premiums.

Other Insurance

Dental coverage is usually not part of your health insurance policy. Dental care may be purchased as a rider to the main policy, however. If not, you can obtain an individual dental policy. Rental car insurance may not be necessary if you already have car insurance. Verify with your insurance agent to what extent you are covered if you rent a car. Regarding travel insurance, if your schedule is subject to change or you're planning foreign travel, insurance can be worth the investment. Buy from an independent company rather than a travel or tour agency. Read the fine print because certain events or items may be excluded. Speaking of fine print, pet insurance is seldom a good deal because of the exclusions that a standard policy usually contains, especially concerning specialized treatments.

In sum, insurance is a way of transferring risk. How much risk you should retain and how much should be transferred to an insurance company is a personal decision. Consider the degree of risk you're able to tolerate, the likelihood of the risk affecting you, and the cost of transferring the risk. As always, check all contractual language, making certain the policy covers you more like a blanket than Swiss cheese, with holes where coverage should apply. Even if your initial reaction is to dismiss coverage because you are young and healthy, when you have children or other loved ones who are financially dependent upon your income, it is financially irresponsible not to purchase disability, health, and life insurance.

Sources and Resources

www.cainc.org (A list of states with risk pools for health insurance.)

www.ambest.com; *www.moodys.com*; *www.standard andpoors.com* (Check the insurance company's ratings on these web sites. Stick with A-rated to ensure that you have a company that can pay your disability claims.)

www.insure.com (Provides quotes for travel insurance.)

www.iii.org/individuals/disability (Disability insurance information.)

www.ssa.gov/disability (Disability insurance information.)

Northwestern Mutual Financial Network: (*www.nwmf.com*) (Disability policies.)

Auto Insurance:

http://articles.moneycentral.msn.com/Insurance/ InsureYourCar/12hiddenWaysToSaveOnAutoInsurance (April 17, 2007)

www.autoinsuranceadvocate.net (State requirement information for liability coverage.)

For Health Care Power of Attorney forms:

University of Michigan Health System: *http://www.med.umich.edu/1libr/aha/umlegal02.htm* (Sample Health Care POA form.)

Family Caregivers online: *http://www.familycare giversonline.com/legal-medical.html* (Sample POA forms for all states.)

National Center for Lesbian Rights: *www.nclrights.org* (Offers Health Care POA information.)

Investment Basics

*"Index funds are going to beat the
results of most investors."*

Warren Buffett

Buy low and sell high. You've heard the adage, but if financial success were that simple, everyone who owns stock
would automatically be multimillionaires. The fact is that
you're unlikely to conquer Wall Street by individual buy-
and-sell stock picks. To do so, you'd have to spend the
time equivalent to an analyst, researcher, and trader combined (and, if you have that much free time on your hands
at your job, you're either going to be laid off or fired, so
you shouldn't be putting any money in the stock market).

Managing a Portfolio

Successful management of your investment portfolio is
based on four fundamentals: (1) diversifying assets; (2)
minimizing costs and taxes; (3) outpacing inflation; and
(4) buying and holding for the long term. For rookie
investors, add a fifth element: stock index funds. Study
after study has shown that stock index funds outperform

111

the average investor and even some mutual fund managers. In short, stock index funds are your best bet for long-term investing success.

Diversification

Unless you love risk, diversification is essential. It balances the ups and downs of the market in an effort to make up for the fact that no one truly knows what the future will bring (hence, the reason it's difficult to know if you're buying a stock when it's really at its "all-time low" or selling when it's really reached its "all-time high"). To diversify, spread your assets over four categories of investments:

(1) Liquid

This is cash. After you've paid off debt, socked away an emergency fund, and maxed the annual retirement contribution, put your money in a money market bank account. If you can't meet the minimum for a money market account yet, a bank savings account is fine. It's not sexy, but it's safe and that's what the purpose of this portion is. This is money that you can convert to cash quickly, if needed. When will it be needed? When you find an investment that is undervalued, as opposed to overvalued or fairly valued. In the meantime, you won't lose your money. You'll save it and earn interest.

(2) Inflation Defense

Inflation affects the power of your money. It's an important factor in calculating whether you'll have enough money in the future to accomplish your goals, especially retirement, and will be discussed more in that Chapter Nine. For now, know that it is an important consideration in your investment strategy. If you can afford it, put some money in items that hold their value when paper money does not. A home, gold, silver, or other real estate investments are typical examples. As you probably know, inflation is the result of the government printing more money when in deficit. But don't make the mistake of assuming a deficit's presence will allow you to predict horrendous inflation. Consider the size of the national debt in relation to the economy as a whole. You don't have to be an economist to understand that if the economy grows by 4 percent and the national debt by 4 percent, the national debt is not dangerously bigger, relative to the economy as a whole.

(3) Deflation Defense

While the analysts and the media focus on inflation, there is a possibility of deflation. Think the 1930s when things were cheap, but no one had any money to buy anything. Cash and a thirty-year Treasury bond are the best examples of a deflation hedge. So, the "liquid money" portion of your investment can double as a deflation defense, too. With the bond, you're locking-in a certain rate for thirty years (for example, 8 percent for thirty years; if the going rate drops to 3 percent, you're deemed the new "It" market watcher).

(4) Affluence Hedge

When a prosperous economy reigns, you want to be in on it and the stock market provides you with the potential opportunity. Notice the word "potential." Essentially, the stock market is legalized gambling. It is not for short-term cash or money you can't afford to lose. For example, if you're planning to buy a home in three to five years, don't put the down payment money in the stock market. For amateurs, the best investment vehicle is a no-load (no sales commission), stock index fund. Invest as much as you can comfortably afford to part with on a monthly basis. You can arrange a monthly electronic transfer to your fund account of a specified amount after you receive your paycheck, just as you can with your money market or savings account.

Selecting an Asset Allocation

Asset allocation involves determining how much money you want in each of the four categories of investment. "Don't put all your eggs in one basket." That's the theory behind diversification, and that's how asset allocation works. When one sector has low returns,[6] the other should have high returns; diversification ensures a balance so a single downturn won't financially wipe you out. Cash, stocks, bonds, mutual funds and cash equivalents (for example, Treasury bills, CD's) will make up a diversified portfolio. Tolerance for risk, age, life events, how much time you have before you'll need the

---

6. A "return" on investments can be income, capital appreciation or both. For example, assume you buy a stock for $100. After a year, it produces $8 in dividends. The income return would be $8 divided by $100=8 percent, or the current yield. If at the end of the next year, the stock is worth $112, it has appreciated by 12 percent (12/100); this is the growth rate. The total return is 20 percent, the sum of the income return and growth rate (8 percent+12 percent).

money, the current status of the market, interest rate decreases or increases and predictions for the future are factors that will help you choose from ultra-conservative to extremely aggressive allocations. Generally, stocks have the highest return and highest risk,[7] bonds offer lower returns and lower risk, and money market accounts are the lowest return and lowest risk.

Different types of investments behave differently. For this reason, when you conduct your annual review of your finances, discussed in Chapters One and Two, consider whether to reallocate your investments once a year, as well as when there is a significant change in the economy. For example, if your stocks had a fantastic year, but bonds were sluggish, you might decide to change to a more aggressive allocation with an increase in the stock allocation. Another practical example is that if bonds did well, but you anticipate that interest rates will rise, increasing the bond allocation would be a mistake. Don't buy bonds when it is anticipated

---

7. **Highest-risk investments:** futures, commodities, limited partnerships, collectibles, real estate investment trusts (REITs), penny stocks, speculative stocks (for example, stock in new companies) and high-yield (junk) bonds. (Note "high yield" does not mean high interest with little risk.) **Moderate-risk investments:** growth stocks (companies that reinvest most of their profits), corporate bonds with low ratings, balanced mutual funds, aggressive mutual funds, rental real estate, annuities, and international stocks. **Limited-risk investments:** corporate, municipal and federal government bonds with high ratings, index mutual funds, and blue-chip stocks (for example, those stocks included in the Dow Jones Industrial Average). The investments are measured against the particular index to which they apply. The Standard & Poors (S&P 500) is the index for 500 of the largest companies in America; Russell 2000 measures the performance of small to mid-cap companies, for example.

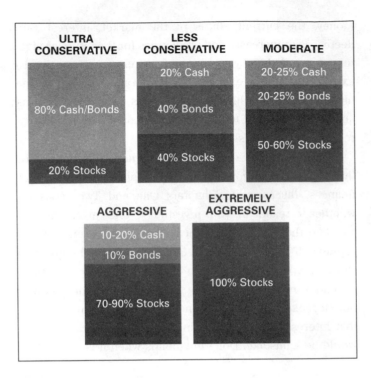

that interest rates will rise because you'll be saddled with a lower than market rate and earning less than if you had waited.

Typically, the younger you are, the greater your financial ability to handle more risk, presuming you have the stomach for it, and don't plan on retiring in your thirties. For example, when you're in your twenties, allocating up to 90 percent to stocks or stock mutual funds is generally appropriate, assuming that the other factors (risk tolerance, time before you need the money, state of the market, and interest rates) fall into place. In your thirties, you may choose a less aggressive position at 70 to 80 percent stocks or stock mutual funds, and adding bonds for stability and income—again, depending upon the other factors.

When you have limited funds to diversify, and need to stretch them over the four categories previously discussed, consider that cash will cover liquidity and deflation. Convertible bonds can provide a fair fixed income in the event of deflation (unless the issuer goes broke) and the value of the bond rises if the common stock (into which it's convertible) rises such as during periods of moderate inflation or prosperity. Likewise, U.S. savings bonds can be relatively liquid, provide a guaranteed rate of interest (which proves good in the event of deflation) and provide for the possibility of high interest (during inflation).

If you anticipate needing to use your money in less than five years (such as for a down payment on a home), the stock market is not the best option. Rather, investing your money in lower-risk vehicles such as short-term bond funds or federally insured CDs would be better suited.

Minimizing Taxes and Costs

Never initiate a transaction without analyzing tax consequences and the costs. Unlike other aspects of investing, taxes and costs are actually something within your control. Tax consequences include short-term capital gains (positions sold in less than one year), long-term capital gains (positions sold after more than one year), dividends, and deferred capital gains (eventual sale of fund shares); the most expensive of these is short-term capital gains. To avoid taking a hit on short-term gains, you either never sell winning stocks or funds held for less than a year, or always offset short-term gains with short-term losses. It is the failure to follow this rule that destroys the after-tax performance of many mutual funds, including hedge funds.

Getting into the Market via Mutual Funds

Mutual funds are the easiest way to invest. Mutual funds invest in stocks and bonds of many different companies. They are lower risk than if you were picking individual stocks and bonds on your own. Starting deposit amounts vary; some may require up to $3,000 and others much less. Some mutual funds are riskier than others, and different funds have different investing objectives, such as income, growth, or tax management.

Load versus No-load

Load is the fee charged by the fund and is stated as a percentage of the amount purchased or sold. Front-end (pay up-front) and back-end loads (pay when you sell) will eat into your profits, which is why no-load funds are more attractive. The benefits of no-load funds are that they offer diversification, professional management, and economies of scale at minimal cost. The fund pools your money with that of others, and invests the resulting millions according to the guidelines published in its prospectus. Stocks, bonds, domestic, international, high-risk, low-risk, tax-free, or taxable: it's all available. No sales commission or back-end redemption fee is charged. When choosing what funds to invest in, ignore the following: (a) those that charge more than 1 percent a year in advisory, administrative, or marketing fees; (b) specialized funds that invest only in a particular sector of the economy, such as gold or technology, unless you believe that you can out-guess the fund manager; and (c) funds that will complement your objectives (for example, long- term growth, tax-free).

Types of Mutual Funds

Below is a summary of the advantages and disadvantages to certain types of funds.

Index

Proper diversification requires twenty to thirty different stocks. You'd likely have to read prospectuses and annual reports on 200 to 300 stocks to pick twenty to thirty winners, and most individual investors don't have the time (or knowledge) needed to do the necessary research. This is why index funds are best for amateurs, as well as those investors who don't have time to spend keeping up with the financial research necessary to track companies, and who don't want to pay a manager to pick stocks. Study after study has established that actively managed conventional-type mutual funds often underperform the stock market. This is another reason a stock index mutual fund is beneficial. An index fund's objective is to match the return of a specified index by buying shares in each stock in that index; the fund tries to replicate the market, whether it's the Standard & Poor's 500, or indexes tracking a single industry or overseas market. Index funds also charge lower fees than actively managed funds. Finally, buying an index fund is almost always a better after-tax choice than buying a conventional mutual fund or hedge fund.

Hedge

The goal of hedge funds is to make money right now by active trading. Tax-wise, this means hedge funds will rack up short-term gains. Thus, the more you or your fund manager trade, the more you have to beat your benchmark to just break even. Hedge fund managers generally charge two fees: management (which usually exceeds 1 percent) and incentive (typically set at 20 percent or more of net profits) versus traditional investments, where only a management fee is charged. High-water marks provide that if the fund loses money, the investors pay only the management fee. However, there is nothing to prevent a manager from quitting instead of working without incentive compensation if the fund falls below its high-water mark. Fund managers, at their core, have the fun (and stress) of gambling with other people's money. Because hedge funds have traditionally been a vehicle reserved for the uber-rich, if your money is invited to participate in one, congrats! However, proceed with caution. As with all other investment opportunities, research the fund management, where your money is going, the tax consequences, and the rate of return.

Conventional

These actively managed funds employ managers and teams of research analysts whose goal is to pick stocks of companies that will outperform their peers. The expense of employing these people increases costs which, in turn, reduces fund returns. Most impose fees and other penalties to discourage investors from buying and selling shares quickly, since this is trading activity that can harm long-term shareholders. It should be mentioned that there can be similar charges imposed at discount brokerage firms that distribute funds with "no transaction fee" settings, as well as by full service brokerages that may charge "contingent deferred sales charges," which apply when you sell certain funds within several years of purchase.

Tax Management

These funds employ a variety of techniques designed to avoid making certain income and capital gain payouts. Do not choose these funds for a "tax-advantaged" account such as a 401(k), however. The argument for choosing tax management funds over others is that they harvest losses that can be used to offset unavoidable long-term gains, and can be more specifically tailored to an investor's specific tax consequences. Critics respond that competent investors will manage their financial life from an after-tax perspective anyway, leaving index funds still the best bet. In fact, several companies have discontinued marketing their tax management funds apparently due to lack of investor interest.

Whether you decide to invest in mutual funds, such as an index fund, or do your own individual stock picks, always analyze the tax consequences. It's the best way to boost your return and for those with an addictive personality, calculating tax ratios can help to curb a stock speculation addict's urge to risk profits for the adrenaline rush of buying and selling.

Avoid Common Market Mistakes

Whether you're an amateur or a seasoned professional, the financial health of your investments can become derailed if you don't keep the following in mind when considering whether to, and how to, invest in the market.

Mania Doesn't Equal Money

It's easy to get sucked into the hype. "Everybody's doing it" wasn't a good justification for your parents to allow you to jump off the roof, and it's not a good reason for investing in something either. For many, the stock market is a snoozer and learning about how it ticks generates yawns. Enter the financial media, devoted to helping you make a profit while entertaining you at the same time. Except, they have to make a profit, too, and their way is to make the market entertaining; otherwise, you won't watch, read, or listen. Tantalizing IPOs, top ten ways to beat the pros, debates about what stocks will be the next Microsoft: the message is the stock market is exciting! Get involved! Move that money!

The reality is that once you've mastered the investment basics and have a good financial footing, frenetic account activity is dangerous. Think about it: every time you initiate a transaction, you can incur transaction fees, taxes, as well as endure the psychological stress of wondering whether it will it go up, and boring your family and friends by complaining about the market when it goes down. Worse, the financial media's focus in their programs and articles is often short-term thinking. Short-term purchases decrease your odds of making a significant profit. Read any article by, or about, self-made billionaire and investment guru Warren Buffett and you'll learn that the most profitable (and predictable) way of earning money is investing for the long-term, not soaking up a financial commentator's short-term stock picks. Long-term equals decades—at least ten years—not months. That's not to say, don't read investment articles, or listen to, or watch the investment shows. They have some good stories: markets soaring, crashing, the latest scams and swindles, underdogs becoming rich or going broke, CEOs doing the perp walk and being marched off to jail. Just keep in mind that bankruptcy, government investigations, fraud, and unbridled success have been part of the market forever—and have even proved a staple for many a lawyer's livelihood! So, don't get too caught up in the entertainment, becoming reactive without careful scrutiny of what, if anything, lies behind the big story or next big stock picks.

Advisors and Predictions

True visionaries are rare. There are probably as many predictors, prognosticators, and financial advisors with methods to psyche out the market as there are investors. In fact, there's an old Wall Street story about an advisor who is walking near the harbor with a prospective client, pointing out all the yachts owned by the successful brokers. "But, where are all the customers' yachts?" the potential customer innocently asks. Silence. Perhaps *The New York Times*' 1986 article, "Leaving the Law for Wall Street," sums up Wall Street's allure best: there's so much money to be made it causes lawyers to bolt from law firms to find jobs in the financial Mecca. That's not to suggest that all advisors, analysts, or brokers are cloaked in greed, but when someone quips about a sure-fire way to earn a phenomenal return on your money, don't be swayed by the slick brochures or a chart illustrating those projected returns. Projected returns are not fact; they're nothing more than statistics, so treat that advisor like an opponent's expert witness. Deconstruct that chart like it's exhibit 1 and interrogate the offeror about the underlying information that went into that chart, specifically, the phenomenal rate of return the offeror is promoting. What are the assumptions that went into those project returns? (Often, there will be no assumptions.) How were the projected returns calculated? Were the projected returns calculated before or after the fees, transactions costs, taxes and inflation? The more phenomenal the return, the more likely it was calculated before all of these adjustments. The goal is to make certain that the data are not being manipulated to paint a rosier picture than what will likely occur if you invest your money. Moreover, a ten-year average of how an investment has performed is only a snapshot. According to an article co-authored by Warren Buffett for *Fortune* in 2001, during the twentieth century, there were three bull markets in which the Dow jumped more than 11 points and three major stagnant markets in which the Dow lost 292 points. In the aggregate, three bull markets lasted forty-four years; the bear markets fifty-six years, leaving more than a century when the Dow's performance was not stellar. The point: it takes decades' worth of information to determine how the market will trend, not a pie chart illustrating projected returns.

Pile On

People think the market is about getting in when a stock is hot or about to soar, then pile everything into it, and earn a windfall when you sell in a few months or years. The problem is that predicting the market is notoriously difficult. From hostile takeovers of the '80s to junk bonds, dot-coms, IPOs, the stock market crash in 2000, and LBOs in between, bubbles burst. When the bubble bursts on a trend, the ride ends, and it always ends badly. Diversification is the safest way to protect your finances.

> Initially diversified, Alec began investing in dot-coms. His stock investment grew to $1.6 million. Overwhelmed by a money-making frenzy, he ignored diversification principles, believed the media hype, and piled all of his money, including his retirement funds and home savings, onto the dot-com ride. The stock plummeted before he could sell it, and his net worth dropped to $52,000.

Asset Classes

It's important to diversify among different types of investments (cash, stocks, bonds, international stocks), but it can be just as important to diversify within those asset classes. In other words, don't put all your eggs (especially if they're your retirement eggs) in one company's basket. For a cautionary tale, you need look no further than the headlines generated by the former Enron employees who went broke putting their retirement money in one company's stock, Enron. Had they diversified their retirement assets, the financial hit they took when Enron collapsed would not have been as devastating.

Sure Things

A remarkable, self-perpetuating truth of accumulating wealth is that you get invited to put your money in sure things, little-to-no-risk investments, designed to make you wealthier. From family members to friends, to hungry financial advisors who read of your new job status, all may call you with the offering for a "sure thing." Whether these are stocks, investment strategies, or entrepreneurial ventures, carefully scrutinize these opportunities just as you would with the four fundamentals of investing ((1) diversifying assets; (2) minimizing costs and taxes; (3) outpacing inflation; and (4) buying and holding for the long term). This is because even if your friend has earned wheelbarrows full of money on an opportunity, it doesn't mean you will, or that the investment is right for the goals you have. Finally, remember the only sure things in life, as Benjamin Franklin said, are death and taxes.

Paying Tax on Someone Else's Gain

In December, mutual funds post their gains and, in turn, pass along their proportionate share of all the capital gains that the funds have realized from selling assets all year. The result: you gain immediate taxable income without increasing your shares' value. The way to escape this scenario is to learn when the fund will post its gain for the year, and then buy your shares after that date.

Insider Trading

Don't. The government will eventually catch up to you. Even if you're smart enough not to leave a paper trail, someone always talks (the person you're in collusion with brags to the wrong person, or curious eyes coveting your unexplainable meteoric financial success anonymously call in a tip to the Feds). No amount of money is worth losing your freedom, family, friends, career, and reputation. The only one who will get rich is the legal team you will have to hire to defend you.

Hiring Help

It's one thing to get advice, but don't trust your money in someone else's hands. When hiring help, understand where your money is going—fees, commission, backload, front-load—and don't give someone the authority to unilaterally sign checks for you. Licensed financial helpers have different titles: advisor, attorney, CPA, financial planner; whatever the title, if you're hiring someone to give you advice on your financial investments, and manage them, they should not be charging more than 1 percent per year of the assets managed.

Make certain that the advisor is not earning a commission from the companies being recommended to you, to ensure objectivity. There are some fee-only financial advisors or planners, which means they are paid by the hour, and are not benefiting from siding with one investment over another. If you are paying on an hourly basis, make certain to learn what and how the financial planner charges before the engagement. Consulting financial advisors can be helpful in complex situations or life events such as a divorce. While seeking a financial advisor can help you educate yourself about investments, you should do your own research, too. For many, it's helpful to develop investment goals and a strategy on your own, then interview and meet with a financial advisor to confirm that you have no issues or gaps in the map you've charted.

Losing Focus

Don't make the rookie mistake of switching in and out of funds, trying to outpace the market. Decide what no-load index fund matches your needs, and invest accordingly, while diversifying your money. Otherwise, you waste time and can drive yourself crazy by comparing how your investments measure up to the market (just as you would comparing yourself to someone else). Instead of getting bogged down on whether your investment is outperforming the market, focus on these four questions: Are you saving in diversified investments? Are you minimizing taxes and costs? Are your investments doing well over time? Are you working toward your goals? If the answer is yes to all four, you're fine.

International Investing

It may be obvious, but avoid investing in areas where the government is unstable, corrupt, or its banking system composed of kleptomaniacs, because it's too difficult for your dollar to outpace their urge to steal.

Spreads and Fees

When it comes to trading stocks—though you're better off sticking with a no-load index fund—there are discount brokers and full-service brokers. The spread is the difference between the price you buy something for and the price you can sell it for. Another way to think of it is as a mark-up the broker will charge for handling a transaction. The bigger the spread, the harder it is for you to profit. Although sometimes there's wiggle room in the spread for the broker to shave a bit off for you, don't invest in a stock that has a wide spread without understanding the handicap this places on your chances of making a profit on the particular stock. Fees are another profit killer. Every advisor and transaction comes with a fee, so analyze the true profit earned after-fee deductions (and taxes) are taken.

An Investment Strategy for the New Investor or Busy Professional

For now, stay away from the institutional investor-type investments (investment vehicles designed for those who are moving money in and out of niche markets quickly) and stick with long-term growth (holding your money in the market for more than ten years). Presuming your age is twenty or thirty-something, and you are comfortable with risk, consider an aggressive asset allocation; otherwise, consider a moderate level. Since a stock index fund will match the growth of the stock market without charging high fees for a fund manager, open a no-load stock index fund such as those offered by Vanguard or Fidelity. Set aside a certain amount a month to deposit; one that won't cause you to lose sleep over whether you're going to lose it. (If you can part with it, 10 percent of your after-tax income arranged as an automatic transfer into the index fund account would be ideal). When diversifying your assets, spread the investment over U.S., international, and bonds. The purpose of an international allocation is so that, if the dollar drops dramatically, or the U.S. economy overheats, the international investments should balance the domestic investment losses. Don't attempt individual stock picks unless (a) you know the particular industry intimately and know that you can outpick the analysts, researchers, and other "experts" (experts is in quotes because, remember, no one can predict the future with 100 percent accuracy), and (b) you're so confident in the company and its product or service that you'd own the whole company, if you could. Annually, analyze whether shifting the allocation in the index fund regarding each type of investment over time is necessary—always keeping in mind inflation, interest rates, and the effect of taxes, if any—to achieve strong gains with minimum volatility. When you've established a good financial footing, and educated yourself on investment vehicles, their diversification qualities and tax consequences, then decide whether it is worth the risk to dive into more complex investment vehicles and strategies. Should you graduate past index funds, when analyzing an investment, make sure you know the business and the product or service it sells, whether the company is competently, efficiently, and honestly managed, and only invest when there's a reasonable expectation for profits, not optimism that the stock will go up. Don't forget to run a check of your client cases to determine whether there are any conflicts in investing that you would have to disclose. Finally, always remember, the market is essentially legalized gambling and you're shouldering the risk. So, above all else, *never* put money in the market if you can't comfortably afford to lose it.

Sources and Resources

Where are the Customer's Yachts? or, A Good, Hard Look at Wall Street by Fred Schwed (Wiley Investment Classics 1940)

The Intelligent Investor (rev ed. 2003) by Benjamin Graham (1st ed., 1973)

The Wall Street Self-Defense Manual: A Consumer's Guide to Intelligent Investing by Henry Blodget (Atlas 2007)

A Demon of Our Own Design: Markets, Hedge Funds and the Perils of Financial Innovation by Richard Bookstaber (Wiley 2007)

"Warren Buffett on the Stock Market," *Fortune* magazine (Dec. 10, 2001)

"Evaluating Exchange-Traded Funds (ETF's)," May 20, 2007, *Wall Street Journal* Online (*http://online.wsj.com/public/article*)

"Bear Stearns to Bail Out Troubled Fund," by Vikas Bajaj, *The New York Times*, June 23, 2007 (*www.nytimes.com*)

"Wells Fargo Fined In Disclosure Case," by Floyd Norris, *The New York Times*, June 27, 2007 (*www.nytimes.com*)

www.morningstar.com (Research investments.)

www.motleyfool.com (Contrary view of investing trends, mutual funds, stocks.)

www.thestreet.com (In-depth look at what mutual fund managers are buying.)

www.dowjones.com (Quotes, abstracts of analysts' research reports.)

www.aaii.com (Information on investments, diversification, and building portfolios.)

For Index Fund Accounts:

Vanguard, *www.vanguard.com* (For a no-load index fund, consider Vanguard 500 Index Fund; Vanguard also offers the Total Stock Market Index Fund (VTSMX) for domestic and other fund options.)

Fidelity, *www.fidelity.com* (For a no-load index fund, consider Fidelity Spartan 500 Index Fund; Fidelity also offers the Total Stock Market Index Fund (FSTMX) for domestic and other fund options.)

Other Sources to Find a Mutual Fund:

www.fundfocus.com

www.quicken.com/investments/mutualfunds/finder

"Money 70: The Best Mutual Funds You Can Buy," (Feb. 2007) (*www.cnnmoney.com*)

National Association of Personal Financial Advisors (NAPFA) (*www.napfa.org*) (To find a fee-only financial planner in your area, consult this web site. Also has helpful periodicals.)

www.savingsbond.com (U.S. Treasury Department for purchasing savings bonds.)

Taxes

*"A fool and his money are soon parted.
The rest of us have to wait until tax time."*

Unknown

Taxes will always be here—no matter what the tax protestors argue, nor the political rhetoric spoken at campaign time. Our country also will always call its tax system "voluntary," though the methods of encouraging your compliance may feel like an involuntary servitude (assessing civil penalties, along with collection via garnishments, seizure, and, in certain circumstances, criminal penalties). This is why what matters in financial decisions is not how much you earn, but how much you will end up with after taxes, because that's really how much money you will get to keep.

The Basics

Tax planning is based on minimizing the taxes you pay. An understanding of Form W-4, exemptions and tax brackets is crucial to tax management.

Form W-4

The IRS web site (*www.irs.gov*) provides a withholding calculator that can assist in determining the correct amount that should be withheld from your paycheck. In the keywords box, type in "withholding calculator." Use this calculator before completing the Form W-4 for your employer instead of committing the mistake of having too much tax withheld from your pay. The general rule is that if you receive a sizeable refund, you have had too much withheld. Even if you are too undisciplined to save money, it's better to have an automatic deduction from your paycheck into a savings account than to let the IRS have year-long use of your money interest-free. Similarly, file a new W-4 if you owed over $100 last year when you filed your return, got married or divorced, became a parent, or lost a dependent that you claimed last year on your return.

Know Your Tax Bracket

In the U.S., our income is taxed progressively, in layers, with each layer of income being taxed at a higher rate. The layers are brackets, and understanding how the tax bracket rates apply to your income is important to determining how much income you can keep every year. In real-life situations, this means analyzing how much would you really earn if you slaved extra hours for a performance bonus, or what the real cost of a mortgage is, after tax, if the interest is deducted, as well as how much of your taxable investment income you can keep. The IRS web site offers forms and publications that illustrate the tax brackets for the tax year. Essentially,

> For illustration purposes, assume three tax brackets:
> 10%, 20%, 30%. The 10% rate applies to income from
> $1 to $10,000, the 20% to $10,001 to $20,000, and the 30%
> to income above $20,000. Brad earns $65,000. The rate
> on the first $10,000 would be 10%, so he'd pay $1,000;
> at $20,000 the rate is 20%, so he'd pay $2,000 on the next
> $10,000 of income earned, and, finally, he'd pay 30% on
> the remainder of $45,000 earned, or $13,500. So, he will
> pay a total of $16,500.

the higher the annual income, the more tax brackets you'll cross.

For tax planning purposes, another way to think of this is the tax rate will tell you the percentage of additional earnings that will go to the IRS. For example, assume Brad, from the above illustration, can earn a $5,000 bonus if he works an extra 500 hours. The federal tax bracket, above, shows his ultimate tax rate is 30 percent. This means 30 percent of that bonus will be paid to the IRS. You would also factor in the local and state tax rate, if any. For example, if Brad's state tax rate was 4 percent, then the combined rate is 34 percent (30%+4%=34%); thus, 34 percent of the $5,000 bonus would be paid to taxes, so working 500 extra hours would really net Brad $3,300.

Itemizing can also save you money when you have significant, albeit reasonable, unreimbursed business or medical expenses. Should you have no or low mortgage interest, itemizing will likely not apply unless you have incurred unreimbursed business or medical expenses, or have made large charitable donations.

Exemptions

Exemptions are deductions from your taxable income. Dependents are exemptions and the IRS web site provides information on how to determine the number of dependents to claim. Exemptions do phase out over certain income levels, however.

Preparing a Return

Even for the most intelligent and educated professional, the thought of preparing a tax return can bring on a headache. However, there are things you can do so the effort won't be so taxing (pun intended), beginning with how you keep track of your finances during the year.

Recordkeeping

Maintaining good records is fundamental to preparing a return, whether you prepare the return or hire-out. Detailed, organized receipts, statements, and other documents should be maintained as if you expect to be challenged and have to provide substantiation to establish the deductions and income; merely maintaining a record of your category totals (income, expenses) is insufficient to survive an audit. Unless there's a reason for the IRS to suspect fraud, it's safe to destroy the back-up documents corresponding to a particular return after six years (from the date of filing the return) have passed. Notice the word "destroy." Invest in a good paper-shredder, because that is crucial to preventing identity theft. Maintain storage (electronic or hard-copy) for records such as closing documents for the purchase or sale of your home and improvements made to it, retirement accounts, and investment documents.

Hiring Out

Tax professionals have differing degrees of education and experience. Generally, the least educated is an enrolled agent or tax preparer, followed by accountants, CPAs, and tax attorneys with the most education. Enrolled agents, tax preparers, and accountants are retained for the basics, while tax attorneys, as well as CPAs, are retained for planning and more complex return preparation. As to the forms, the IRS web site provides information concerning what tax and information returns must be filed, along with instructions, the due dates, and publications that can be ordered for general requirement information.

For an educated professional, the substantive and technical preparation of a Form 1040EZ doesn't require hiring out. If you don't want to put pen to paper, there are software programs that are available to streamline return preparation. Typically, the user is prompted with a series of questions (similar to those that would be asked if you were face-to-face with a preparer). Then, the program calculates the amounts owed, and produces the finished product based on the information you supplied. Preparing a Form 1040EZ probably isn't worth the monetary investment in software, however, or the fee for a tax preparer.

Likewise, for an educated professional, hiring a tax preparer or accountant may not be worth it if you're filing a Form 1040 for an uneventful financial year. As an educated professional, you are capable of reading the IRS form instructions and determining what new laws, if any, apply to your personal situation for purposes of preparing a tax return. It becomes financially worth it to hire-out the preparation of your returns if you simply find it too much of a time-consuming hassle to prepare them. After all, paying $100 to a licensed tax professional to prepare and file state and federal returns for you when you could be billing your time at $250 an hour is good economic sense. Tax preparation fees are also deductible. Either way, the more organized and detailed your records, the better. It saves you time if you do the preparation. Organized recordkeeping also saves you money if you hire-out because a tax professional will require less time to prepare the tax return and may charge less.

If you're self-employed, quarterly calculations and preparation of self-employment income may prove more time-consuming, and retaining an accountant can be worth it. For returns involving complex investments or business matters, consider retaining a CPA or tax attorney unless you have an accounting or tax background. For example, if you're fortunate to receive the perks enjoyed by CEOs and a handful of other top executives such as the personal use of company aircraft and cars, country club memberships, or housing and relocation costs, you may likely find the perk triggering an IRS bill, so it should be included in taxable income. The more complex your finances, the better to consult an attorney with the particular expertise in the substantive area of tax law necessary to help you comply with the laws.

Don't File Early

Don't file your tax return early. Generally, taxpayers who file returns early (well before the "Taxgiving Day" of April 15), have a greater likelihood of being randomly selected for an audit.

Discriminant Function System (DIF)

The Discriminant Function System (DIF) is why much has been written about ways to avoid an audit in return preparation; specifically, ways to out-psyche the DIF because the IRS uses it to select returns for audit. Briefly, the DIF is the IRS' scoring system for elements that appear on your return. For example, if you've reported more business-related deductions than the IRS deems normal for someone with your income, your return is going to get some extra points (extra points are not a good thing). If the total score is greater than the IRS guidelines, the computer selects your return for review. If an agent determines that the return requires an audit, that's when you are contacted.

Dealing with the IRS

According to IRS Publication 1, the mission of the IRS is to "provide America's taxpayers top quality service by helping them understand and meet their tax responsibilities and by applying the tax law with integrity and fairness to all." This may be difficult to believe when you receive an ominous envelope containing confusing correspondence spit out by the IRS computer with only a toll-free phone number, which, when called, records your discussion after you've spent 45 minutes listening to elevator music while waiting for an IRS employee to answer the line.

Nevertheless, every lawyer has a purpose (at least, that's what the law school enrollment stats suggests), and tax litigators are no exception. If you have no experience dealing with the IRS, give a call to your legal brothers and sisters who routinely negotiate with the IRS before trying to battle the IRS on your own. That being said, because there is inevitably someone who goes it alone, here is some general guidance.

For some IRS inquiries, all that may be required to resolve the issue is a written response providing information or documentation concerning a forgotten Form W-2 or 1099. Other matters may be more complicated. Obviously, the more complex the issues, the more reason to retain a tax professional with the appropriate level of experience and expertise to help you. If you don't want to pay an accountant, attorney, or CPA to help you, at least consider investing in an IRS procedures book that details how to handle audits, dispute assessments, and seek refunds. The IRS bureaucracy has very defined divisions, each with employees responsible for handling certain duties and tasks and only those duties and tasks. More importantly, each level of the IRS has very specific procedures that must be followed, and substantive law that will apply to the particular dispute. One mistake could prove fatal to the success of your case, resulting in

> Because Dan was a lawyer, he represented himself
> in an IRS audit, disputing the IRS' assessments of taxes
> and penalties up to the IRS Appeals Division. After filing
> suit in court, he learned that he had committed costly
> IRS procedural errors when the government moved to
> dismiss Dan's case.

your losing the battle before the war you wanted to wage ever began. (Hence, the reason tax litigators exist.)

If You Can't Pay, Still File the Return

When you can't pay the tax shown to be due by the due date for filing the return, you should still file it, or at least, file a request for an extension. Not filing by the due date can add up to 25 percent to your tax bill in the form of late-filing penalties. You are not without options in negotiating payment; however, all of them will require providing the IRS with accurate and detailed financial information. More information can be found on the IRS web site concerning the forms that will be required for completion before the IRS will consider discussing a payment plan with you (for example, Forms 433, 656). Should you own assets or have savings, expect the IRS to respond that you should use them to pay, or apply for a loan and use the proceeds to satisfy the tax owed. Obviously, if the problem in paying is that you did not have enough withheld from your paycheck, file a new Form W-4 with your employer so that the error is not repeated on next year's return. As with other matters, dealing with the

IRS in negotiating a payment plan will likely be more successful (and easier) if you consult a CPA or tax litigator if you have no previous IRS dispute experience.

IRS Notices, Demands for Payment

IRS collection actions are serious business. When the IRS has already assessed taxes, penalties, and interest against you, that's when you'll receive notices and demands for payment, and eventually, a visit from a not-so-friendly revenue officer assigned to collect the tax liability. The options of an installment agreement or offer-in-compromise may be available to you. Again, the IRS web site describes these options in detail. However, if you lack experience with the IRS, consult an attorney who routinely practices with the IRS for your jurisdiction.

Strategies for Minimizing Taxes

Reducing your adjusted gross income, increasing your deductions, such as with mortgage interest and charitable contributions, and taking advantage of any credits to which you are entitled are the avenues for minimizing taxes. Highlighted below are four common approaches to achieve such an accomplishment: tax-deferred investments, tax shelters, real estate, and asset placement.

(1) Tax-Deferred Investments

These are used to postpone paying income taxes. A retirement account is the most typical example. Retirement accounts are the easiest way to grow your money while shrinking your taxes. In fact, the best way to reduce your adjusted gross income is by maxing out on your retirement contributions. The higher your combined (local, state, and federal) tax bracket is, the better to incorporate investment tax-deferred vehicles into your portfolio. In contrast, the lower the tax bracket, the greater likelihood you can realize better after-tax returns from fully taxable investments.

(2) Tax Shelters

While many shelters can be based on unsound interpretations of the Internal Revenue Code, some are legitimate opportunities to invest in potentially lucrative deals while getting a tax break. Generally speaking, tax shelters are evidence that CPAs, financial planners, and tax lawyers are an entrepreneurial and customer service-oriented bunch. This is because tax shelters will always exist—in some form, name, product, or structure—as long as client demand for them exists. When you have earned enough money to become a potential client, remember this rule: *never* invest in a deal solely for its tax benefits. If you are audited, the IRS will examine the investment from an economic perspective, and that's how you should, too.

A way to determine a tax shelter's actual profit potential is by measuring the potential after-tax return against the after-tax cost. By doing so, you can compare the cost of a tax shelter opportunity with other investment vehicles such as stocks and bonds that are acquired with after-tax dollars. Also, factor in how long it will take to get the yield from the after-tax dollars. For example, a three-to-one return ($3 of cash received for each $1 invested) will likely not pass muster with the IRS if it takes several years longer to realize the full profit. Bottom line: If the deal wouldn't be worth the risk for you to invest without the tax benefits, then don't do it—unless you're comfortable with the shelter's likely triggering an IRS audit, and the corresponding vacuum on your time and money that an audit can bring.

As a general rule, whenever anyone proposes a "tax-free" investment, be cautious. Often marketed as legitimate investments designed to legally avoid income taxes, "tax-free" vehicles generally are viewed with skepticism by the IRS. The typical scenario occurs where the proposed structure falls within the technical confines of the Internal Revenue Code, thereby making it legal until the U.S. Treasury Department, IRS, and Congress eventually fix the loophole that is causing the "tax-free" result. Thus, a potential investor's concern becomes twofold: how long before the government catches on, and what are the consequences to an investor when it does? Because there are circumstances where the IRS will exercise its right to retroactively issue regulations designed to correct a perceived abuse, these concerns become good questions to ask, along with seeking a (second) opinion letter from an independent tax lawyer about the proposed transaction.

(3) Real Estate

Homeowners are allowed to deduct the mortgage interest from their taxable income. Generally, under present law, you can keep up to $250,000 ($500,000 married) of profit when

Chapter Eight

the home is sold, without paying any taxes on the gain. Not everything associated with home ownership is deductible, however. Association fees and improvements are a common deduction mistake; these expenses are not deductible. However, keep the records for improvements because, if you sell, those expenses will be added into your basis. Concerning other real estate investments, be aware that changing tax laws no longer result in depreciation expenses and tax-loss deductions as an automatic boost to the rate of return. Specifically, incurred operating or tax losses may not be deductible, so research the tax (and diversification) benefits before investing in real estate.

(4) Asset Placement

This strategy is based on the fact that different investments generate different tax treatments under the Internal Revenue Code. The after-tax, inflation-adjusted return for each investment is analyzed so that assets are placed in an overall portfolio structure that maximizes profits while minimizing taxes. In essence, the diversification and tax advantages (or disadvantages) are analyzed before investing. This strategy becomes especially important when you have graduated to high-yielding, volatile, or complex investment structures generating capital gains and losses.

In sum, there are as many tax-planning methods and tax-saving strategies as there are articles and books that you can research to determine which method is best for your situation. Consulting with tax attorneys and CPAs is also recommended, especially for developing advanced planning methods or strategies for high incomes. However, when you become a high-income taxpayer, you'll likely learn that aside from maxing out on retirement contributions, there are generally not enough legitimate ways to reduce taxes.

Sources and Resources

www.irs.gov (Go to search and key-in "Tax Scams—How to Recognize and Avoid Them.")

www.turbotax.com (Offers tax preparation software.)

Tax Preparation Books:

Ernst & Young-publishes tax preparation book annually for the Form 1040; PriceWaterhouseCoopers publishes tax preparation book annually for the Form 1040.

Federal Tax Litigation by Susan A. Berson (Law Journal Press 2001)

"Ask Questions, Look for IRS Red Flags Before Investing In Tax Shelters," by Susan Berson, *Kansas City Business Journal* (April 7, 2006)

"IRS Collections Are Not Put Off By Offshore Assets," by Susan Berson, *Practical Tax Strategies* (December 1999)

Retirement Planning

"Too much of a good thing can be wonderful."
Mae West

When it comes to money in retirement, having too much of it will be a wonderful thing. These days, for many in retirement, the setting sun begins to rise again. Reawakened ambitions, second careers, travel, volunteering, or becoming firebrands for causes about which they're passionate—all of these activities require a retiree to have a steady flow of income to fund them. At some point, (hopefully in much later years), healthcare and physical-care options will likely take financial priority. Simply put, how comfortable you are in your retirement years depends on your money and health. Money also will likely dictate where you live, and the activities you participate in, so careful retirement planning is important.

The Basics: Figuring Out How Much Money You'll Need during Retirement

Most Americans will spend an average of twenty-five years in retirement, which means you'll need to have between ten to sixteen times your salary saved. For a more specific calculation, there are many calculators available on the Internet to help you determine how much money you will need, and they are referenced in the Appendix. Before you use them, however, determine your likely sources of income, anticipated healthcare needs, and how you might want to spend your retirement days.

Income Sources

The possible sources of income for most retirees include: 401(k), IRA, company pension, savings, investments, and employment. Generally, if you can rely on having at least three of these sources, you should have a comfortable retirement; meaning you can afford the daily living expenses necessary for your lifestyle.

Health Insurance Needs

Health insurance is always a major concern. Once a person reaches 65, Medicare theoretically kicks in, but you'll need supplemental insurance for what Medicare doesn't cover. Affordable healthcare is only available for those with no medical conditions, and, after 65, it's rare not to have been diagnosed with a physical ailment or medical condition that requires periodic attention. Thus, the bad news is that you must financially prepare for your health insurance premiums to rise as you grow older, as well as the prospect of needing long-term care insurance mentioned in Chapter Six. The good news is that taking care of yourself now can pay off later. Regularly exercising, quitting bad health habits, and maintaining a healthy weight, are all things you can do now to try to keep fit, and to help maintain the lowest premiums possible.

Don't Count on Social Security or Medicare

When calculating the likely income sources during retirement, don't factor in social security or Medicare. This is because the oncoming crush of 78 million retiring baby boomers will likely crash the Medicare trust fund by 2019, and the social security trust fund by 2041, (unless Congress and the White House find an agreeable cure). So, be prudent and plan as though there will be no social security benefits in your future.

Goals

Finally, though they may likely be developing over the next twenty to thirty years, consider your retirement goals. Ponder where and how you want to live, including what you'll do with the luxury of all that free time. Relocating to a sunny climate, owning a second home for a winter retreat, donating time and money to a nonprofit, traveling perpetually from exotic locale to exotic locale: the world can be your oyster if you plan right. Don't be the 39 percent of retirees who responded in a 2007 Fidelity Research Institute survey that they underestimated the amount of their spending and expenses. When you pen your retirement goals, they should match the lifestyle you would like to have twenty, thirty, or forty years from now, whenever it is you anticipate retiring.

Inflation

Before discussing retirement investment strategies, an understanding of the effect of inflation on your retirement savings is necessary. Inflation works against your investments. When you calculate the return on an investment, you'll need to consider not just the interest rate you receive but also the real rate of return, which is determined by figuring in the effects of inflation. With the exception of the '80s double digit inflation rates, the average rate of inflation has been 2 to 4 percent, according to the U.S. Bureau of Labor Statistics. As mentioned in Chapter Seven, inflation is an important factor when considering your investment strategy. At first glance, an inflation rate of 4 percent might not be of overwhelming concern, until you consider its application to your purchasing power. For example, 4 percent inflation over twenty years translates to the value of a dollar decreasing to $0.44. Over a twenty-year period, a $0.41 postage stamp will be $0.87. Applying that to a big-ticket item: A $23,000 car may command a $50,000 price tag in twenty years. This is important when considering your financial goals because it can reduce the value of your current salary. For example, a $90,000 annual salary will have the buying power of only $86,400 next year if you did not earn a raise to compensate for the 4 percent inflation rate.

Types of Retirement Plans and Accounts

Defined-contributions plans, Individual Retirement Accounts, and Keogh Plans are the types of retirement vehicles available. (If you work for a corporation, you may have a defined benefit plan known as a pension. The traditional pension plan will not be discussed because it is becoming a thing of past, as it places much of the retirement savings responsibility on the employer.) These investments are a way to grow your money, while saving taxes. With few exceptions, they offer the power of compounding interest while you pay no taxes on your contributions or their earnings until you withdraw the money after age 59-1/2. (Withdraw before that age, and it will result in the IRS imposing ordinary income tax and an early withdrawal penalty.) By age 70-1/2, you have to start withdrawals, or face a 50 percent penalty of the minimum distribution amount.

Defined-Contribution Plan

Most employers offer some form of a defined-contribution plan. Your contributions (and those of your employer, if applicable) are kept in an individual account in your name. The advantage of this plan is that you can decide how your money will be invested. The plan will set the terms of how frequently you can change the allocation on your investment choices. If you change jobs, you can take the money with you and rollover to another retirement vehicle. The most common plans include: 401(k) (private employers), 403(b) (non-profits, tax-exempt employers), and 457 (government, nonprofit employers). Others are money-purchase plans, profit-sharing plans, thrift or savings plans (TSAs), and savings incentive match plans (SIMPLEs).

(1) 401(k). Employer-sponsored retirement plan whereby participating employees receive a tax break for saving for their retirement. Contributions are deducted from your paycheck, before your taxes are calculated. You don't pay tax on the earnings until you withdraw them—presumably at retirement—at which point, your investment grows faster because your untaxed earnings benefit from compounding. Some employers may match a percentage of your contributions, (for example, .50-$1 to every $1 you deposit) though the law applies a cap on the matching amount. The employer match is usually subject to vesting after you've been there a few years. Otherwise, you're always 100 percent vested in your contributions. Contribute to the 401(k); don't walk away from free money. Limits on the contribution are adjusted by the IRS every year. Other limits for low versus highly compensated employees may also apply, unless your employer has adopted a safe-harbor provision for all eligible employees.

(2) 403(b), 457. These plans operate much like a 401(k), except that in a 457 plan, the account is funded solely by the employee's contributions. No employer matching contributions are permitted.

Individual Retirement Accounts (IRA)

There are several variations offered by financial institutions, mutual funds, or brokers. Like a 401(k), the IRS sets the contribution limits annually. If you do not have access to an employer-sponsored plan, open one of these types of IRAs, detailed below. Otherwise, max-out your contribution to the employer plan first. Nondeductible contributions may still be made, and the earnings on those contributions are exempt from tax until the money is withdrawn. For any nondeductible contributions made (except for Roth), keep records so you won't be taxed again when you withdraw. Withdrawing nondeductible funds before 59-1/2 will cause the IRS to treat the withdrawal as a proportionate blend of both the nondeductible and deductible contributions so a penalty in some proportion may apply.

(1) Traditional IRA. Whether contributions to an IRA are tax-deductible depends upon your income, and whether you are participating in a qualified retirement plan at work. (If your contributions are not tax-deductible, then you should consider a Roth, discussed next.) Presuming your income isn't greater than the annual limit set by the IRS, if you (and your spouse) do not participate in any employer-provided retirement plan, you can deduct the contributions made to the IRA. Like the 401(k), the money grows tax-deferred until you withdraw them at retirement, when they are taxed at your regular income tax rate. You have up to and including April 15 to make a contribution for the previous tax year, just make certain you make contributions before you file your income tax return because the IRS will verify the contribution date.

(2) Roth IRA. Contributions to a Roth are not deductible, but the earnings are never taxed. Unlike the traditional IRA, where you're required to withdraw a minimum amount each year once you turn 70-1/2, a Roth has no such requirement. The IRS does place limits on the amount you can contribute based on your income, however. You should delay distributions from Roth IRAs for as long as possible, because the income that builds up is tax-free.

(3) Simple IRAs, SEPs. A Savings Incentive Match Plan for Employees (SIMPLE) IRA is for businesses with no other retirement plans and with fewer than 100 employees. Your contributions and earnings are tax-deferred, and the IRS requires the employer to match contributions, with certain limitations on the matching amount. Simplified Employee Pension (SEP) IRAs are similar to SIMPLEs except only the employer can contribute. The disadvantage is that you have no control over how much money goes into your plan. If you are participating in either a SEP or a SIMPLE, you can still invest in a traditional or Roth IRA.

(4) Keogh Plan. These plans are for people who have self-employment income. Though the IRS no longer uses the term "Keogh," many still refer to profit-sharing and money-purchase plans as "Keoghs." In a money-purchase plan, the same contribution each year is required even if you haven't made any profits. The contributions amount is limited by the IRS. Likewise, with profit-sharing plans, the contributions are also limited, but the amount can change each year.

Rules of Retirement Investing

Follow the rules summarized below when investing for retirement.

Start Early

You'll realize the maximum appreciation in your investments, and recoup a loss should there be any disappointing investments. Even if you can only afford $10 per month, do it now! After forty years, that monthly $10 deposit, assuming 9 percent interest, will put you $40,056 closer to a more comfortable retirement.

With Youth Comes Agility, Be Aggressive

The longer you have to invest, the more that time will make up for any short-term losses. The corollary to this is that the younger you are, the more aggressive the investment can be. If you don't plan on retiring within the next thirty years, the bulk of your retirement account should be in stocks or stock index mutual funds, because you have several decades before you'll need the money. (By contrast, if you were saving to buy a home in a few years, the down-payment money would be better in a conservative investment such as a certificate of deposit or short-term bond fund.)

Save 10 Percent

Generally, you should save at least 10 percent of your annual adjusted gross income toward retirement, regardless of whether the contributions are taxable.

Portfolio Allocation

Be conscious of your overall portfolio's asset allocation. Analyze the diversification and tax consequences of your retirement investments, alone, but also as the retirement investments fit in with your overall portfolio asset allocation.

(1) Stock allocations. The general rule is, the longer the investment horizon, the more risk that can be tolerated. This means the assets in your retirement account have the longest horizon in comparison to other assets in your portfolio because it will be decades before you withdraw them. But diversification is just as important to retirement funds as to your overall portfolio. So, don't invest everything in one stock. For overall portfolio asset allocation purposes, be aware that capital losses realized inside a retirement plan are not deductible.

(2) Liquidity allocation. Don't put all your cash in the IRA. Keep some outside the plan for emergency, due to the early withdrawal ordinary income tax and penalty.

(3) Bond allocations. Tax-deferred, compounded earnings are the benefits of placing certain bonds in your retirement account. High-yielding bonds, in general, produce current income each year. Don't place tax-free bonds (such as municipal bonds and Series EE bonds) that are sold by federal, state, or local governments in retirement accounts. By putting these tax-favored instruments in a tax-deferred vehicle, the income earned becomes taxable when you withdraw money from your retirement plan, effectively converting a tax-free investment into a low-earning, taxable one. (Series EE are subject to no state income tax, yet are taxed at the federal level but usually only when you redeem them.)

Juggling Debt

Being in debt isn't permission to blow off retirement investing. It does mean that once the credit cards are paid off, you must max-out on your retirement contributions and play catch-up by making (nondeductible) IRA contributions.

Emergencies

Only as a last option, consider withdrawing from your IRA if you're certain to have enough cash to replenish the withdrawal by opening another IRA within sixty days. You can do this only once during a twelve-month period.

Age-Appropriate Retirement Investment Strategies

Invest in a no-load stock index fund. On average, a well-chosen stock index fund compounding under the retirement canopy should outperform an investment in bonds or life insurance. If your investment horizon is at least twenty to thirty years off, you can financially handle an allocation of 80 to 90 percent of your retirement money to a broad-based U.S. stock index fund with the remaining 10 to 20 percent to an international fund. As discussed in Chapter Seven, if you don't want to (or can't) take the time to actively manage your retirement account, the index fund approach gives you a good financial base. If you will be manually adjusting your asset allocation (rather than using a fund such as Vanguard

Age-Appropriate Allocation: As You Age, Reallocate Money to Conservative Investments			
Age	**US Stock**	**International Stock**	**US Bond**
20s	70%	20%	10%
30s	62%	18%	20%
40s	55%	15%	30%

Target Retirement Funds and Fidelity Freedom Funds that can automatically adjust the asset allocations for you as you age), select your asset allocations making certain that your U.S. stock funds have a mix of large-cap, medium-cap and small-cap stocks, as well as a mix of value stocks and growth stocks. The age-dependent strategies below are also worth considering.

Twenty-somethings

Sign up for your employer's plan, save enough for the matching contribution, if available. If there is no employer retirement plan, enroll in a Roth IRA, and deposit the annual maximum amount. For example, in 2007, the maximum contribution was $4,000. At 8 percent for forty years, that $4,000 investment would find you a tax-free millionaire by retirement age. If you can't save the maximum, save what you can. For asset allocation, consider the chart above for manual allocations. Otherwise, buy one fund, such as the Vanguard Target Retirement Funds or Fidelity Freedom Funds, which can make the age-appropriate allocation automatically for you.

Thirty-somethings

Pump up the retirement investments. When you receive a bonus or raise, put as much as you can afford in retirement savings. (If a lump-sum deposit of your bonus is too austere, consider a gradual monthly increase.) Want to retire early or reduce taxes? If you've already maxed your contribution to the work plan, open an IRA, preferably Roth. Start saving just $3,000 at 8 percent, by age 70-1/2, you may have $840,000. Boost it to $3,500, and it may be $980,000. Don't let one stock dominate your retirement savings, spread the stock allocation over several different players, as illustrated in the chart, above. This is true even if you've been working at a company in which you've invested your retirement savings; no one stock should ever exceed more than 10 percent of your portfolio. Don't let your financial health be so dependent upon a single company's health. Finally, if you're about to vest (that is, keep more of your employer's contributions), financially, it is usually best to wait to change jobs.

Forty-somethings

If you've consistently maxed-out retirement contributions for the past ten to fifteen years, you should be on track, and need only adjust the allocation in accordance with the previous chart, and consider opening an IRA in addition to your employer plan. Conversely, if you've neglected your savings, you must make the sacrifices necessary to max-out on contributions to your employer plan *now*, and open an IRA, for catch-up savings. If you've been rising up the career ladder, you may not satisfy the income requirements for a Roth (at least until 2010, when anyone can enroll), so a non-deductible IRA is your option. Unconvinced that you need another retirement vehicle? Consider a 2007 study by Putnam Investments and Brightwork Partners: 46 percent of retirees over the age of 61 who returned to work said that if they had it to do over again, they would have also saved money outside their employer retirement plans. Finally, if you're considering saving for a child's college education instead of your retirement, consider this: there are no scholarships for retirement. So, don't make yourself one of those 46 percent of retirees who have to return to work.

Regardless of age, diversify your assets, especially those within the stock index fund you choose for your retirement dollars. Automatic deductions to the retirement account are always the most disciplined way to save. Finally, whatever your age, the sooner you start saving, the better. Reaching your retirements goals rests entirely on your shoulders. Don't put saving off, because whatever your retirement goals turn out to be, there is one certainty: retirement will cost money.

Sources and Resources

Savings and Retirement: To help you get a better idea of how much money you need, you can go to *www.choosetosave.org* and use the Employee Benefit Research Institute's free Ballpark Estimate worksheet.

www.livingto100.com (Calculate when you might check out so you can help gauge how much money you'll need to live and also determine how to better your health.)

http://www.bloomberg.com/invest/calculators/retire (Retirement calculator.)

http://cgi.money.cnn.com/tools/retirementplanner/ retirementplanner (Retirement calculator.)

Low-Cost Index Funds:

Vanguard (Vanguard Extended Market Index fund (VEXMX)) gives exposure to both large-cap and small-cap companies, across a wide variety of industries. The Vanguard Total International Stock Index fund (VGTSX) gives international exposure. An initial $3,000 investment in the VGTSX funds is required, so, given the typical $4,000 annual IRA maximum, you may need to focus on the broad U.S. VEXMX fund first, and then add on the international fund in a future year.)

T. Rowe Price Funds (For a lower monthly or quarterly investment, consider that it allows periodic investments of as low as $50. It has a low-cost, U.S.-based extended market index fund (PEXMX), as well as an international index fund (PIEQX).)

www.retirementplanner.org

Social Security: *http://www.socialsecurity.gov*;
Medicare: *http://www.cms.hhs.gov* (Trustee's report
dated April 23, 2007: social security paying out more in
benefits than it collects in payroll taxes starting in 2017.)

www.ssa.gov (Should the government radically fix
the siphon on the social security system, you can visit
the Social Security Administration's web site's planner
and calculator section for factors that influence the
benefits received.)

"Build the Big Sum You'll Need," by Walter Updegrave,
Money Magazine (*http://money.cnn.com/2007/03/09/
magazines/moneymag/retireearly_savings.moneymag*)

"Fill Your Riskiest Gap: Insurance," by Walter Updegrave,
Money Magazine (*http://money.cnn.com/2007/03/09/
magazines/moneymag*)

"Retired, Then Re-Energized," by Margaret Graham
Tebo, *ABA Journal* (April 2007)

www.myplanafter50.com (The site serves as a portal
to information on topics such as financial planning,
employment and health for fifty-plus.)

Life Events

"A pessimist is one who makes difficulties of his opportunities and an optimist is one who makes opportunities of his difficulties."

Harry Truman

The adage that life is what happens while we're making plans should encourage you toward financial preparedness. No one can predict what the future will bring, but having your finances ready can make life's events (both good and bad) less tolling on your bank account and, in some circumstances, your emotional state when they occur.

Job Loss

Terminations and layoffs: few people who've been in this situation started the job feeling their position was this insecure. Planning for a potential job loss focuses on health and retirement issues. For your financial health, maintain the emergency fund, discussed in Chapters One and Two, and learn what happens to your benefits. Specifically, termination for cause results in COBRA ineligibility.

When a Fortune 500 corporation slashed its outside counsel roster from 400 to twenty-three law firms, Marc's firm was not one of the lucky twenty-three. When the work dried up, the firm laid him off, even though he was a capable third-year associate. Since his former colleagues' resumes were saturating the market, his job search to land a comparable salary lasted for months.

As discussed in Chapter Six, without health insurance, an accident or illness could financially break you. Health insurance becomes an expense for which you'll have to save, and increase your emergency savings fund. Retirement plans present other choices: rollover the funds to an IRA, or possibly to your future new employer's plan, or, depending on the balance in your account, keep it in the former employer's plan. Finally, keep your resume updated with references ready.

Job Change

On average, attorneys will change jobs at least twice during their career; sometimes for better pay or experience, other times because they have no choice for employment. Health concerns dictate that you review the benefits you'll have at the new job versus those needed for purposes of whether COBRA is applicable. Retirement options are the same as those discussed in the "Job Loss" section; however, vesting issues may take the forefront. If you are about to vest in the

> **I Hate My Job!** For readers new to the working world, this may be a shocking concept, but there may come a day when the job or career path you have chosen is not everything that you hoped it would be. Worse, despite your best efforts to make your working environment challenging and enjoyable, the only thing keeping you there is the paycheck. If you aren't debt-free and armed with an emergency savings fund, the employer's paycheck dangling in front of you becomes the stick instead of the carrot. Being debt-free with an emergency savings fund will give you the greatest luxury of all: the freedom to say, "I'm not doing this anymore." You can quit, take a break, or switch to another occupation altogether, without sacrificing food and shelter.

employer's retirement plan, hold off on the job change. Bouncing from job to job before vesting can significantly set you back in saving for your retirement needs.

Burnout

Not to dampen your enthusiasm, but there's a reason stress management books are best-sellers among lawyers. The legal world can present an environment that nurtures burnout. Against the backdrop of enormous time pressures, the higher your salary, the more pressure on productivity and hours, which can exacerbate the very quality-of-life issues that can make even the most ambitious and talented people unhappy.

> Quitting a lucrative associate job at a high-powered firm, Bob, a skilled New York lawyer, opted for a self-imposed two month sabbatical on the high seas. Fulfilling a life-long dream of learning to sail a 54-foot sailboat, offered him the advantage of not only mastering a new skill, but gaining a fresh perspective on teamwork, leadership, and the practice of law. Returning recharged, physically fit (and tan), he accepted another high-paying job with an equally high-profile Wall Street firm.

Leaving the law is a path some attorneys may follow. To ensure that building wealth remains possible, paying off debt, maintaining an emergency fund, and consistently maxing-out retirement contributions should be accomplished before the legal career ends. That's not to say that if burnout happens to you, another lucrative career isn't possible. There are many occupations where a law degree and background is helpful. Still, without an emergency fund established, you'll rapidly incur consumer debt, forcing you into a job you'll likely hate.

Sabbatical

Some firms sponsor paid sabbaticals, although, before you can be eligible to participate you have to be anointed partner, and then, toil for at least seven more years. (Sort of like dangling the carrot on the stick if you're already an overworked associate or new partner.) If you've been slaving in a job that doesn't offer such a future reward, the idea of a self-imposed sabbatical may be appealing.

Should the traditional partnership track be your personal Holy Grail, voluntarily quitting your job or seeking a temporary leave of absence will postpone it. However, when you're good at what you do, you normally don't have to boast about it, people know it. If you're the type of person who works so that you're not just better than the competition, but are known as the only person who can do what you do, your career may not be damaged by taking a self-imposed sabbatical for a month or two. In contrast, the same might not be true about your financial health unless you adequately prepare. Save enough to cover your annual retirement contribution, daily living expenses (so you don't charge up the credit cards), and to sustain your emergency fund before you embark on a sabbatical to volunteer for Greenpeace, stump for a political campaign, explore the world, or fulfill a life-long dream. How to approach this with a current employer? Firms that have joined the sabbatical trend find that partner sabbaticals can make for a more productive (and loyal) partner, and the same should be true for associates. Obviously, this argument is much more persuasive when it isn't spoken by a first-year associate, so if you're still early in your career, consider why you want the sabbatical. If you're unhappy at work, it may be that you really want a permanent sabbatical from the law, or simply your employer; therefore, taking a self-imposed temporary sabbatical will only be a Band-Aid, not a cure for the real problem.

Relationships and Finances

Financial preparedness extends to relationships. Certain relationships come with more financial responsibilities than others, and keeping your financial house in order becomes even more important when others are financially dependent on you.

Moving In Together

Next to someone appearing desperate or too needy, talking about how to spend money can be a romantic mood-killer. Nevertheless, if you're serious about a long-term relationship with someone, the money discussion is crucial to both emotional and financial happiness. The agenda for the money discussion does not include bragging about how fat your paycheck is (or whining about how slim). Rather, take the Spender Quiz in the Appendix, and let the discussion unfold. Inevitably, couples who are unable to honestly discuss financial issues and reach moderate compromises (when they differ) are in for either a tumultuous relationship, bankruptcy, or both. So, if you're serious about sharing your life with someone, let the romance temporarily wane for an hour, and discuss your attitudes toward money and how it is spent and saved.

Ironically, few cohabiting lawyers actually have a cohabitation agreement for themselves—though lawyers make a mint off people who move in without a cohabitation agreement. If you're one of these cohabiting people, though you may rationalize that, as a lawyer, you can argue your way out of anything, put it off no more (especially if you have a psychologically sound friend in your trusted circle who is telling you that your beloved is not for you). Without a cohabitation agreement, you're sabotaging all the hard work you've done in creating a financial plan. Think of it in billable time: One hour at your computer drafting up contractual terms versus months consumed by fighting over who gets the love nest and Fido, if domestic bliss should end.

Finally, consider whether a healthcare proxy or healthcare power of attorney is needed. (This allows someone to make your medical decisions for you when you can't do so.) This is important for couples living together, especially same-sex partners, because some hospitals will not automatically accord visitation privileges to nonrelatives in emergencies. This document spells out who can visit you, who can set the visitation list, and who the patient is designating as family. Note that while a HIPAA authorization healthcare power of attorney can give your significant other authority to make decisions on your behalf, a separate document usually has to be drafted that authorizes your significant other to see, and get copies of your medical records under the new regulations for HIPAA. This is a necessity for filing insurance claims, obtaining second opinions, and making informed decisions.

Getting Hitched

Whether you're having a wedding or a commitment ceremony, before you say "I do," discuss finances. Money—controlling it, hiding it, spending it, saving it—is a primary reason couples divorce. Even if you don't view divorce as a likelihood, money issues can turn an otherwise happy union into a battleground. If you're contemplating tying the knot, save yourselves the arguments, heartaches, and worries by discussing your goals, and agreeing on a plan for how your combined finances will be earned, saved, and spent. If you find that your soon-to-be is carrying a horrendous debt load and a credit rating to match, it is financially wise to consider a long engagement until it is improved. Even though it may be emotionally difficult to postpone the wedding bells, consider that a couple beginning a union with a struggling inability to keep creditors at bay is statistically likely to hear the rustling of divorce papers in their future.

Want an argument favoring being a kept man or woman? Consider that getting married normally increases a couple's tax bill, unless they structure it so that one of the soon-to-be spouses isn't generating income. A second personal exemption deduction becomes available to the working spouse, and both spouses can make annual IRA contributions, potentially decreasing a married couple's total adjusted gross income. On the other hand, if both of you will be working, review each employers' health coverage and determine which health plan offers better benefits. Do the same review with retirement accounts. Ultimately, merge your recordkeeping and bill paying systems together into one, concise, yet thorough method.

Finally, a prenuptial agreement becomes a must-have wedding gift when you live in a community property state or may inherit valuable (or sentimental) assets (or the psychologically balanced person in your trusted circle is advising you to run). Even if your betrothed has promised to never

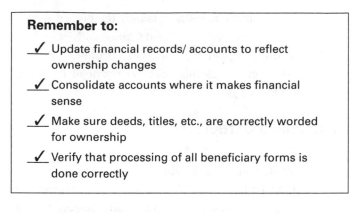

Remember to:

✓ Update financial records/ accounts to reflect ownership changes

✓ Consolidate accounts where it makes financial sense

✓ Make sure deeds, titles, etc., are correctly worded for ownership

✓ Verify that processing of all beneficiary forms is done correctly

take something you hold near and dear, a person's memory can fade after living in luxury, especially when the prospect of it ending is near. Put it in writing.

Getting or Giving the Boot

Just like investing in the wrong stock, when you invest in a relationship with the wrong person, it often doesn't pay off. However, when JLo recorded "Love Don't Cost a Thing," it must have been before she divorced, because the primary question will be, "How much is it gonna cost me?" After the emotional trauma, child, or pet custody issues, the bottom line is money. This book is not advocating that committed couples include divorce in their financial plan. Rather, this section is for those who are already contemplating it, going through it, or have already done it. Despite having a good divorce lawyer to advise on the custodial and property issues, most divorced couples seldom come out financially ahead when the ink is dry on the order of dissolution. To ensure that any financial setback is only temporary, during, or after, a divorce, consult a licensed financial advisor who is certified in divorce planning aftermath, if only to confirm that your strategy for getting back on financial track and building wealth is a good practice.

Becoming a Caregiver

Many professionals may find themselves sidelined, at some point, to handle family responsibilities. Whether caring for an elderly parent or having a child, becoming a caregiver can sap your finances if you haven't financially prepared for it. Some trend-setting employers offer flexible work schedules and telecommuting that allow you to fulfill both home and work responsibilities. If you don't have that option, preparing a budget that allows you to hire help or quit working will keep your promising financial future intact. On average, it can take up to five years for every one year you are not working to recapture lost benefits, savings, and to get up to speed on the pay scale when you opt back in to the workforce. Therefore, protect your retirement by continuing to max-out your annual contributions.

Concerning your aging parents, be proactive and have a talk about planning for their long-term care needs. Most children also end up handling their parents' estates when they die. Yes, the inevitable is a sensitive subject, but there's no need to become the Addams Family. View the situation as you would any other client problem that you've been asked to analyze. You're simply troubleshooting and developing a plan for contingencies. Gently broach the topic with your parents, have the talk, make a plan, and, hopefully, the subject will not be reopened for a very long time. Still apprehensive? Estate attorneys earn thousands assisting beneficiaries and trustees in deciphering unkempt financial records; thereby reducing the estate's value and prolonging the nightmare for the surviving loved ones. One uncomfortable talk can spare you this situation.

Regarding children, it's guaranteed they will cost you money (and time). As important as emotional maturity is to being a good parent, financial preparedness is equally important. Save for parenthood just as you would any other goal. (Note: if your employer's attitude is that parental leave is a sabbatical, re-read Job Changes/Job Loss section.) The IRS Child Tax Credit Worksheet determines whether you are eligible for a tax savings. The Uniform Transfers to Minors Act (UTMA) has also been promoted as a tax-saving measure by shifting investment income onto your child's tax return. There are disadvantages. For example, capital gains will have to be recognized at some point, and the funds are taxed at the parents' marginal tax rate. Also, the asset will be counted if your child seeks financial aid. You'll also lose custodial control over a UTMA when the child is eighteen or twenty-one. A better way to teach your child about savings and taxes may be, when your child starts a part-time job (presuming the wages aren't destined for a college fund), to open a Roth IRA in the child's name for investing some of the child's income. If you can afford it, sponsor a matching program for every dollar the child invests. A $1,000 investment at 8 percent, beginning at age fifteen, results in $815,000 by age sixty-five—more than twice the amount of a worker who starts saving the same amount at twenty-five. In the event you have difficulty severing the financial purse strings to your bundle of joy (or vice versa), avoid the mistake of sacrificing your financial stability to support older (physically and mentally capable) children. Forty-five percent of working parents have a child twenty-five or older whom they financially support. Worse, 38 percent are saving less for retirement because of it, and 29 percent delay retirement, according to a 2007 survey from research firm Putnam Investments and Brightwork Partners.

A final word about caregiving: pets. Furry or otherwise, they cost money (and time). As with everything financial, consider whether there's room in your budget (and schedule) to provide food, veterinary care, and pet-sitting services before committing.

Other Events

Financial management bolsters good opportunities that come your way and can also soften the blows. Preparedness is key to enabling you to act when either occurs.

Becoming Your Own Boss

Sometimes there are rewards for not following the herd. But it takes more than guts to strike out on your own; it takes financial building blocks, too. If your business development efforts have built your client receivables, don't think you can bank on immediate receipt of those receivables when you leave a firm to start your solo career. It's not uncommon for firms to pay out receivables to a departing attorney (especially a partner) over a number of years. Protect your financial health by paying off debt, maintaining the emergency fund and maxing-out retirement savings. Before your solo career thrives, it's important to your financial success for you to have a sound financial net worth: both so you live comfortably and can obtain financing should you need it to run your operation. Otherwise, your practice will run you instead of you running your practice.

Second Home

A second home for vacation or eventual retirement conjures up idyllic images of a spacious beach house or ski lodge, with your fabulous friends driving up for the weekend, their black Range Rovers and Mercedes arriving on your manicured drive, lining up in rows like a box of chocolates. That beautiful retreat can turn into a House of Blues if you don't understand that it is a full-time financial commitment. Depending on the property, your current mortgage, property taxes, insurance, and maintenance could likely all be doubled, so budget accordingly.

Widowed

Sadly, becoming widowed is not a status reserved only for old age. Following these tips can help alleviate the financial stresses during a time of grief. First, take two or three months off, allowing yourself time to grieve. Second, assess what your assets are, where they are, and define your goals and prepare a budget, as discussed in Chapter Two. (If you haven't been the financial gatekeeper who has paid the bills and maintained the records, start learning now.) Finally, financial preparedness before a crisis occurs will ease anxiety and save you money. It's not enjoyable to contemplate, but if your significant other is diagnosed with a terminal illness or becomes a fatality in an accident, it's in your best interests to have as much done beforehand. Have a financial conversation at least once a year, especially if you are not in charge of the family finances, so you know what you have and where it is (for example, assets, bank accounts, insurance policies, and agent's phone numbers). Copious forms will require completion before money will be distributed from investments and insurance, yet bills will have to be paid, decisions made, such as selling the home, handling family care, and day-to-day liquidity. All will require attention, and having your records in order will help you get a solid footing.

Estate Planning

As an attorney, you know the consequences of not planning for the inevitable. Yet, statistically, a surprising number of attorneys don't have the basic documents executed, presumably because they're pressed for time or they have difficulty coming to grips with their own mortality. In any event, make it easier on your loved ones and have the list of documents below in order. Potential embarrassment should motivate you on this one: think of your mourners speculating about the wisdom of a lawyer who dies without a will!

(1) Wills, trusts (for children, pets) shared custody agreement (domestic partners)

(2) Healthcare proxy, power of attorney

(3) Bank, brokerage account, retirement statements

(4) Safety deposit boxes-check whether sealed upon death and need to have a co-owner

(5) Insurance policies and agent contact information

(6) Tax returns

(7) Credit card and other debt information

(8) Locations of secured places (safe, safety deposit box)

(9) Email accounts and passwords

(10) Property records for real estate, cars and other major assets

Sources and Resources

What Can You Do With A Law Degree, by Deborah Aaron (Niche Press)

www.newlywedfinances.com

www.kathleengurney.com (Psychologist offering advice to couples about money.)

"Couple Learns The High Price of Easy Credit," by John Leland, *The New York Times,* May 19, 2007 (*www.nytimes.com*)

Society for Human Resource Management (SHRM) Data June 2007 (11 percent of large companies offer paid sabbaticals; 29 percent offer unpaid sabbaticals); *Fortune* 100 Best Companies to Work For 2006 (Two law firms that offer sabbaticals made the list.)

"After Baby, Boss Comes Calling," by Lisa Belkin, *The New York Times,* May 17, 2007 (*www.nytimes.com*)

Family Caregiver Alliance (*www.caregiver.org,* 415-434-3388. Offers information for caregiver concerns, newsletters (English, Spanish, Chinese), and online support group.)

The National Alliance for Caregiving (*www.caregiving.org,* 301-718-8444. A national resource center that provides information on elder-care conferences, books, and training for professionals.)

National Association of Area Agencies on Aging (*www.n4a.org*, 202-872-0888. An advocacy group for local aging agencies, also offers The Eldercare Locator (*www.eldercare.gov*, 1-800-677-1116), a service that provides local resource and referral organizations, which in turn, recommend home healthcare aides.)

The American Association of Homes and Services for the Aging (*www.aahsa.org*, 202-783-2242, publishes free brochure on how to choose nursing home or assisted-living facilities, a directory of continuing-care retirement communities and information on long-term care insurance.)

"Lessons of the AM Law 100," *American Lawyer* (May 2007)

www.flextimelawyers.com (Matches lawyers with short-term projects.)

"The Tyranny of the 2nd Home," by Tracie Rozhon, *The New York Times*, May 18, 2007 (*www.nytimes.com*)

Giving Back

"It is everyone's obligation to put back into the world at least the equivalent of what they take out of it."

Albert Einstein

Many lawyers participate in the much-needed pro bono efforts involving everyday landlord/tenant matters, immigration issues, as well as newsmaking wage disputes and headline-grabbing DNA exonerations. There are other creative ways for lawyers to give back, however. No matter how little you think you have, there is always someone who has it worse. For those with charity at heart, it's understood that the donation of time and money is a privilege and an obligation to one's community. For others, donating can provide a tangible benefit in the form of charitable deductions on a tax return. Whatever your impetus, giving back to your community provides a happy return. Share your expertise, time, and money. Figure out what skill you have to offer and the cause to unite it with, then, get started.

For New York lawyer Bari Zahn, creating
livingbeyondBelief.org had a personal impetus.
She started the foundation in honor of her deceased
uncle to educate high schoolers about HIV/AIDS,
and has received world-wide acclaim.

But, I Have No Money

Maybe you don't, but you know how to use a phone, the
Internet, and pound the pavement. Fundraising is always
needed. You can send letters and emails—both from the comfort of your home or office—soliciting donations. If you're
especially adept at raising money, consider starting a foundation. Many lawyers have started nonprofits to fill a void they
saw in their communities. The Wills for Heroes Foundation
began with a lawyer filling a local need to provide no-cost
estate-planning documents to emergency workers and now,
with the help of a second lawyer, it's gone national. Bottom
line: If the community needs your help, you help. Don't be a
cosmic ingrate.

But, I Have No Time

Maybe you do. Volunteering can take as long or as short a
time as your schedule permits. There are thousands of organizations with varying needs and time commitments. Also,
your effort need not be purely altruistic. You'll be getting
back a return on your investment of time, though it will be
intangible. For example, consider board membership as a

Chapter Eleven

resume-builder. Once a month, you lend your legal expertise and meet with other civic-minded and community oriented people by serving on a nonprofit's board. It can also boost your presence with an employer when an organization is entrusting you with its future—encouraging the employer to trust you with additional responsibility.

Or, how about a quick cure for a bad day? Instead of diving into a pint of Haagen Dazs, Scotch or [insert your poison here], try taking a thirty-minute break to help someone. Add in another thirty minutes for your commute time, and before you respond, "I don't even have thirty minutes to spare, let alone sixty," consider that you'd likely spend at least thirty minutes buying and consuming your poison, and another thirty minutes venting to someone in your trusted circle by whining or complaining about your problem without developing a resolution.

It doesn't have to be an earth-shattering, time-consuming effort: manning a hotline or the soup kitchen's food service line, reading, drawing, or playing soccer or kickball at an after-school program, or assisting with taekwando at a senior

> By day, Bernie Knight is an award-winning Washington, D.C., attorney, but one evening a week he has put his Masters of Psychology degree to work by volunteering with an organization that helps traumatized children recover from having a parent murdered. He's an example that a mere one-hour contribution can make a life-long difference in someone else's world.

center. If you prefer to keep face-time at the office, help a starving artist analyze a royalty contract. If you prefer to take a stroll and think about your problems, stop by the animal shelter and check-out a dog for a walk. You can think and walk at the same time, can't you? Aside from the temporary reprieve a volunteer-break will give you, you'll likely get a pick-me-up, and you'll gain a new perspective on your problem after helping someone out with theirs.

Volunteering can also keep you young. A study by Community Service Volunteers (CSV) found volunteering had improved health, confidence, sense of purpose and self-development for their study subjects. Need more evidence? Consider a report from Yale School of Public Health that maintaining positive thoughts and actions can keep you young. What better exercise than volunteering—making a positive contribution to someone or something else—to help you maintain those positive thoughts?

Get Inspired

Don't let a big "but" stop you from making a difference. You don't have to go it alone. It can be a firm-wide effort. Organize your colleagues, and build a family a Habitat for Humanity home, or walk, run, and trot in a charity marathon. Some firms have their own charitable foundations and fund employee-driven community projects. Get involved.

No one expects you to stand around and sing Kumbaya, but if you've been given good fortune, you've got to share it. The legacy we leave is how we live our lives every day. Right now, your good fortune may take the form of intelligence, opportunities, money, or all three. Show your appreciation for what you have by sharing it. Always remember, life is a series of choices. You can choose to be a good example of benevolence, generosity and goodwill, or a horrible warning of arrogance, gluttony, and greed. Choose wisely.

Sources and Resources

American Institute on Philanthropy: *http://www.charitywatch.org* (Rates charities.)

www.irs.gov (Lists legitimate tax-exempt charities and not-for-profits.)

"An Unusual Rep: Firms Compete to Win Pro Bono Projects," by Jill Nawrocki, *American Lawyer* (March 2007)

"Volunteering Keeps You Young," BBC News, Dec. 8, 2004 (*http://news.bbc.co.uk*)

"Many Happy Returns," by G.M. Filisko, *ABA Journal* (April 2007)

"Liberty Under Law," by Karen J. Mathis, *ABA Journal* (May 2007) (Discusses ABA Youth at Risk Initiative.)

2007 Bottom Line Health Newsletter, by Becca Levy, Ph.D. from the Yale School of Public Health

Spender Quiz:
What Kind of Spender Are You?

The questions below are designed to provide an illuminating snapshot of the emotions and thought processes that may drive your buying decisions. Circle the answer that applies.

You're going grocery shopping, do you:

    (1) have a list that you stick closely to of items to purchase based on a look in your fridge and cupboards;

    (2) have no list, but a general idea of what you need to buy;

    (3) buy what looks appealing.

Waiting in line at the grocery store, you:

    (1) browse the magazines, but don't buy them;

    (2) grab one or two things, but not completely load up the tab;

    (3) load up on magazines, candy, whatever you see that you may want.

Your friend begs you to go shopping, you don't need anything but you go:

    (1) purchasing nothing, even though you see something that you want, because you'd rather allocate your money toward your goals and the "want" is not one of them;

    (2) purchasing whatever you want so long as it doesn't break your bank account;

    (3) purchasing whatever catches your eye regardless of considering whether you truly need it, and, if you don't have the cash to cover it, you know that you can charge it, because you have an available balance.

Your microwave broke, do you:

(1) get on the Internet and research the prices and models of the stores in your area to find one you like that fits within your budget;

(2) go to a store where you normally have received good deals, look around, and buy the one you like;

(3) go to the first store you see that sells microwaves and buy one.

Payday at work, and the money is direct deposited into your account. The first thing you do is:

(1) plan the expenses for the next couple weeks to figure out what needs to be paid and what can be put into the emergency fund or savings;

(2) relax, knowing that you'll figure out what to do with the money later;

(3) celebrate by treating yourself to something new, like the new arrival your favorite store just emailed you about that you find appealing.

You've been thinking about getting a dog, do you:

(1) research the type of breeds, their temperaments, and requirements that would be best suited to your money, temperament, and time constraints, then get on the Internet and research animal shelters in your area for animals that are available for adoption before actually deciding whether a dog is the right fit for you at this time;

(2) have an idea of what you can afford, and the type of breed you want, so you adopt one without any further research;

(3) buy the most expensive pup you like from a breeder because that means it's the healthiest.

Your secretary has been telling you how much she and her recently unemployed husband love their new big-screen TV »they bought with a financing offer of no payments until next year. You've been wanting a big screen, so you:

(1) research what is the best-quality big-screen and the prices, determine that you don't have enough saved for that yet, and continue saving, putting off the purchase until you can pay cash for it;

(2) buy the cheapest big-screen that fits within your savings, even though the salesperson provides you with a credible report that shows it won't last more than two years;

(3) decide that if your secretary and her unemployed husband can afford it, so can you, and finance the big screen.

It's summer, the air conditioner has broken and you have to replace it, because you're living in Nevada where it's 110 in the shade. You drain the emergency fund to pay for it, and now your friend wants to go out to dinner at a wonderful French restaurant. You:

(1) are tempted and explain you'd love to go with her, but will have to pass because you don't have any disposable income to spare after replacing the a/c. She brings over a bottle of wine and you cook whatever is in the fridge;

(2) invite her over for dinner, picking up a couple of yummy things at the grocery store, and eat-in at half the price of the restaurant;

(3) accept, figuring you'll order something cheap, and, if the restaurant she's chosen is going to cost you more than $20-$30, you'll just charge it.

When you receive your credit card bill, you:

(1) pay the full amount because you don't purchase anything unless you will have the cash to cover it at the end of the month when the bill comes;

(2) pay back more than the minimum, but not enough to pay it off because you can't afford other living expenses if you do;

(3) pay the minimum so you can have more cash to play with during the next couple of weeks.

You just arrived home after buying a $30 item from a store thirty minutes away, only to learn it doesn't work. You:

(1) immediately return it, or schedule time tomorrow to do so, and get your money back;

(2) put it aside, deciding you'll return it the next time you're near the store. Then, you forget about it, and, when you remember, it's too late, so you settle for a store credit;

(3) decide to forget about returning it. It's not worth the hassle for $30.

When you hear someone talk about money, you:

(1) have enough to pay living expenses and your savings account, and think that so as long as you carefully watch what you spend your paycheck on, you'll be okay;

(2) become a bit tense because, while you're meeting your living expenses, you're unable to save consistently, and wish you had more in the emergency fund;

(3) complain that you never have enough even after you received a raise.

When you shop, you:

(1) buy things when you need them, prepare lists ahead of time; and try to remember to ask yourself whether

what you are considering is something you really need versus something you just want;

(2) buy things that you want and need, but only if you can afford it;

(3) buy things with the motto, "I'm in the hole so deep, what's a few more dollars matter," or "life is short, if you want it, buy it."

In general, when you have a big purchase, you think:

(1) I'll start researching for the best quality and price;

(2) forget research because it's all a wash;

(3) who needs research, money matters are boring and I'm swamped. I'd rather spend my free time on a more exciting outlet.

You need a suit for a meeting with clients. At the store, you find a quality suit, though the price is a bit over your price range, but is made to last. So you:

(1) buy it, pledging to reallocate money from another category in your budget, such as your monthly latte fund to cover the cost;

(2) opt to buy two cheaper suits for the price of the one suit, because, even though the material is cheaper on the two cheap suits, you'll add two new suits to your closet instead of just the one. Plus, since they're so cheap, you can always buy more suits when the fabric gives out;

(3) leave it hanging on the rack because, if it doesn't have the highly coveted designer label, and Hollywood isn't wearing it, you're not buying it. So, you pay the extra money to special-order something, knowing that it will be out of style by year's end.

ADD UP THE NUMBER OF "1," "2," and "3" ANSWERS

TOTALS: _____1 _____2 _____3

MOSTLY "1's": Investment Shopper

Generally, you're a smart shopper. You don't fall for the bells and whistles that are unneeded, and you don't buy cheap things that won't last. Things that have stood the test of time hold the greatest interest. You're in a place where you can truly appreciate quality over flash and fads. Let other people fall for the disposable, mass-produced look, you're unique. Once you have a clear vision of what you want, you make a plan to get there. You likely break down big goals into smaller steps that make them feel more attainable. With each small step completed, you feel the satisfaction of accomplishment, and it helps maintain your motivation to stay on budget and move toward accomplishing your financial goals.

MOSTLY "2's": Impulse Shopper

Impulse Shopper: You may understand that it's possible to look hot without melting your credit cards; however, even though you may only charge small amounts, or withdraw small amounts of cash, your money seems to leak out of your pocket almost instantly. When money is in your wallet, or in your bank account, you feel either compelled to, or are fine with, spending it.

Psychological studies suggest that many impulse shoppers range from frustrated "creative" types who have imaginations that can fuel their shopping sprees, to individuals with low self-esteem who may feel that they do not deserve to be prosperous.

When you hand over your cash, you are handing over responsibility for your life or decision-making. If it still doesn't sound like you, then maybe you are the deprived child. If treats were the cure for blue days, or if you were deprived as a child and always dreamed of getting yourself the reasonable things you were

194

denied, you could be associating the purchase of inconsequential nothings with feeling good. Unfortunately, that good feeling likely ends when you look at your bank account balance. The good news is that while impulse shoppers may dig themselves into debt, they can recover.

Try viewing the process of getting out of debt and managing money as a challenge, and use your creativity to find more satisfying ways to fill yourself up than mini- shopping sprees. Extending your creative ways to your financial world will give amazing results. If you can start to see saving your money as a challenge, then you may have fun finding creative ways to do so, and it can help you become more materially comfortable. Otherwise, being in debt for you will be like having a large ship steered by a very small rudder. You're staying afloat, and moving, but not going very fast and not getting very far ahead. If it helps to equate getting out of debt and building a savings program like a work project, treat it like a challenging document production or due-diligence task.

Initially the mountains of documents and electronic information can be overwhelming, but when you break it down into smaller steps, completing the project becomes more attainable. Break your debt down into small pay-offs, or your savings program into small deposits. With each small step completed, you feel the satisfaction of accomplishment. As you break your debt down into small pay-offs, while building your savings up each month, with each small step completed, you'll feel confident and motivated to continue becoming debt-free and build your wealth.

MOSTLY "3's": Emotional or Vanity Spender

Emotional or Vanity Spender: You're using retail therapy to fill a void. "I deserve to treat myself" or "If I only had that, my life would be better" are the classic lines. Whether it's insecurity, acceptance, anxiety, or loneliness, the sooner you realize that money can't buy you a sense of peace for any of these feelings, the sooner you'll be able to become debt-free, financially stable and build wealth. Until then, you'll continue to use credit cards to supplement your income, regardless of whether you're earning $60,000 or $1 million, and you'll never get to where you need to be for financial success. Your purchases are largely the creation of vanity, rather than a logical need. Money can't buy love, or so goes the song. But, it also can't buy true respect or acceptance.

Psychological studies suggest that emotional shoppers tend to search for these intangibles with the tangible. Splurges may be triggered by an insecurity or guilt, with the true motivation being reassurance. When you don't feel validated at work or home, if your first thought is to buy something to make yourself feel better, in lieu of spending, try substituting something else that normally makes you happy. Some emotional shoppers may also have a tendency toward the "Daddy Warbucks" attitude: price is no option when it comes to my friends or family. Just because your love may be equivalent to Cartier doesn't mean that you have to break your bank account to buy a gift there, especially when you're charging it and won't have the cash to cover it when the statement arrives. Nor does it mean that the expensive gift will guarantee the return of true feelings toward you. For you, dealing with debt and risk is like anything else in life, you have to know where the line is that you won't cross, because there's always going to be someone bringing out some emotion that is ready to push you over that line, and if you haven't decided where your line is, you're going to get yourself in serious financial trouble.

For all types of shoppers, a good software program can revolutionize, and streamline your budget planning to help you stay on track and achieve your financial goals.

Financial "To Do" Checklist

☐ (1) Determine financial goals ("If you fail to plan, you plan to fail.")

    ☐ Short-term (within a year)

    ☐ Medium-term (1-5 years)

    ☐ Long-term (over 5 years)

☐ (2) Establish a recordkeeping system, and destroy discarded receipts and statements.

☐ (3) Budget:

    (a) Take 10 percent off your monthly take-home pay before developing a budget to meet necessary expenses;

    (b) Apply the 10 percent to maxing-out your retirement contribution and establishing an emergency savings fund, unless credit card and student loan debt exist;

    (c) If debt exists, pay off credit cards. If employer has matching retirement program, budget so you can participate in it, and pay off credit cards. Analyze student-loan debt options, along with computing interest rate and tax deduction to determine whether payoff is appropriate. Once credit cards are paid off, after your paycheck is direct deposited, have 10 percent directly routed from your checking account monthly toward: (i) maxing-out the annual retirement contribution; (ii) emergency savings equal to six months' pay. Maintain the emergency fund in an interest-bearing federally insured account. When the credit card debt is paid off, and (i) and (ii) have been accomplished, allocate funds toward investment account or other goals, such as down payment for a home or purchasing a car.

☐ (4) Credit cards: Know interest rate and pay off balances on monthly basis.

☐ (5) Car: If financed, accelerate payments on debt to eliminate interest being paid to creditor instead of your goals.

☐ (6) Home loan: Consider (i) shortest term; (ii) 20 percent down payment; and (iii) if you are buying less than five years from now, put money in certificates of deposit or short-term bond fund for maximum interest earned.

☐ (7) Insurance: Protect your assets, including your ability to earn income.

☐ (8) Investments: (i) Diversify; (ii) maintain low costs and taxes; (iii) no-load index funds offer the broadest diversification, and, if you can invest on a monthly basis, market fluctuations will matter less to long-term growth. The indexes are: Wilshire 5000 Index (large, mid and small cap U.S.); S&P 500 Index (Large cap U.S.); Russell 2000 (Small cap U.S.); MISC EAFE (broad international stock index); Lehmann Aggregate Bond Index (broad U.S. bond index); (iv) allocate money in a combination of U.S. stock funds, international stock funds, and U.S. bond funds. Make certain that U.S. stock funds have a mix of large-cap, medium-cap and small-cap stocks. Also, make sure that U.S. stock funds have a mix of value stocks and growth stocks.

☐ (9) Conduct annual review of net worth, credit report and diversification allocations.

About the Author

Susan A. Berson learned about the importance of financial vigilance while living on a government lawyer's salary when she began her career in the Attorney General Honors Program with the United States Department of Justice, Tax Division, in Washington, D.C. Her financial experience expanded when she entered private practice in 1998, becoming a partner with an AmLaw100 law firm, and later resigning in 2005 to start her own boutique firm which is now called The Banking & Tax Law Group, LLP (*www.banktaxlaw.com*). Throughout her career, she has been intrigued by the financial management secrets that explain why some lawyers (and clients) appear to grow money, while others continue to struggle in the weeds despite earning hundreds of thousands of dollars, if not millions, annually. Serving on various boards and committees, she has also been active in fundraising and volunteering for community and charitable organizations.

Graphics courtesy of Brian J. Laughlin

Index

American Association of Retired Persons (AARP), 90

Asset placement, 144, 147

Bankruptcy
disability and, 40
FICO score factor, 67
generally, 48-49
last resort, as, 61
See also student loans

Bonds
generally, 115, 116, 117, 118, 126, 130, 146
junk, 125
retirement account and, 158, 160
savings, 117, 158

Buffett, Warren, 111, 123, 124

Cash flow, 17, 23

Child Care Provider Loan Forgiveness Program, 43

COBRA (Consolidated Omnibus Reconciliation Act of 1986), 92, 165, 166

College education fund, 24

Credit bureaus, 46-48, 62, 66, 69, 71

Credit cards
debt, 7, 21, 27, 78
estate planning and, 179
FICO score and, 66-69
generally, 15, 24, 28, 29, 53-63, 82, 84
grace period, 55, 68
interest rate, 66
piggybacking, 70
retirement and, 159

Credit report, 42, 47, 48, 66-70, 84

Disability
insurance, 93-95, 99
student loan and, 40

Discriminant Function System, 141

Emergency fund
establishing, 6, 92
generally, 7, 23, 25, 27-30, 82, 166-169, 177

Enron, 126

Federal Family Education Loan Program, 36

Federal PLUS loans, 41

FICO score, 66-71, 76, 83, 84, 106-107

Financial advisors, 123-124, 126, 127-128

HIPAA (Health Insurance Portability and Accountability Act of 1986), 92, 171

Home equity loans, 57, 65-66

Individual Retirement Accounts
  generally, 97, 150, 153, 154-156, 158-162, 166, 172
  Keogh Plan, 153, 156
  Roth IRA, 155-156, 160, 161, 175
  SEP, 156
  simple IRA, 156
  traditional IRA, 155

Insurance
  credit life, 64, 100
  life insurance, 95-99
    borrow against, 57
    term, 96-97, 98
    variable universal, 98
    whole life, 97-98

Interest
  accrual, 44-46
  deductibility, 50, 136, 144, 146
  difference between forbearance and deferment, 44
  graduated repayment, 44-45
  money-market account, 112
  retirement plans and, 153
  whole-life insurance, 98

Interest rate
  annual percentage rate, 83
  bonds and, 115, 117
  consolidation loans, 35-38, 41
  credit card, 54-57, 59, 60, 62
  credit score and, 66-68
  financing car, 63-64
  forbearance, 44
  generally, 17, 21, 50, 59
  home equity loan, 57, 65
  incorrect, 49
  investment strategy, as part of, 130
  mortgage, 76-77, 79-81
  refinancing, 58, 81, 85-86
  retirement accounts and, 58
  return on investment, 152
  student loan debt, 7

Internal Revenue Service (IRS)
  Child Tax Credit Worksheet, 175
  collection actions, 142
  dealing with, 141-143
  Discriminant Function System and, 141
  form instructions, 140
  generally, 137

recordkeeping and, 138

retirement plans and, 153-156

tax shelters and, 145-146

web site, 136, 139, 143

Managed-care plans, 90-92

Medicare, 150-151

Medicare Prescription Drug, Improvement and Modernization Act of 2003, 105

Mortgages
  adjustable rate, 77, 79-81
  debt-to-income ratio, 77-78
  FICO score and, 67, 84
  fixed rate, 79-81, 83
  generally, 2, 23, 76-86
  interest deduction, 76, 86, 146
  monthly expense as, 15-16, 26
  refinancing, 85-86

National and Community Service Trust Act of 1993, 43

Net worth balance worksheet, 2-3

Prenuptial agreement, 172

Public-interest lawyers, 46

Real estate investing, 146-147

Recordkeeping
  computer-generated, 14, 29, 30
  errors in, 49
  generally, 13, 28, 138-139, 140, 172

Replacement cost coverage, 102

Retirement
  contributions, 7, 25-27, 29, 30, 168, 169, 174, 177
  financial goal as, 1, 4-5, 151
  inflation and, 152
  planning, 149-164
  plans
    borrowing from, 58
    defined contribution, 153
    401(k), 58, 121, 150, 153, 154
    403(b), 153, 154
    457, 153, 154
    job loss and, 166
    tax-deferred investment as, 144-145

Sallie Mae, 35, 36

Social Security, 47, 95-96, 151

Social Security Administration, 95

Stafford loans, 37, 44

Stock index funds, 111, 112, 114, 119, 122, 128-131, 157, 159, 162

Student loans
 consolidation
  generally, 34-38, 44
  time frame, 37
 default
  generally, 46-47
  reinstatement, 48
 deferment
  bankruptcy and, 49
  compared with forbearance, 42, 44
  default and, 47
  generally, 37, 39-41
 forbearance
  bankruptcy and, 49
  compared with deferment, 42, 44
  default and, 47
  discretionary, 43
  generally, 42-44
  mandatory, 43
 generally, 1, 7, 33-51
 grace period
  bankruptcy and, 49
  generally, 33, 34, 37
 standard repayment schedule, 34, 44

Tax-deferred investments, 7, 144, 155, 156, 158

Tax shelters, 145-146

Taxes, 135-148
 brackets, 136-138, 145
 capital gains, 117-118, 127, 147, 175
 exemptions, 138
 Form W-4, 136, 143

Teacher Loan Forgiveness Program, 43

Title IV (Higher Education Act), 42, 47, 48

Uniform Transfers to Minors Act (UTMA), 175

U.S. Department of Education, 36, 42, 47, 48, 49